GW00579638

DEWSBURY BOY

Growing up in the West Riding
1925 to 1946

by

Cliff Moiser

British Library Cataloguing in Publication Data

Moiser, Cliff

Dewsbury Boy: Growing up in the West Riding 1925 to 1946

I. Title

ISBN 0 946873 13 5

Copyright © Cliff Moiser 1994

First published in Great Britain 1994 by Basset Publications

All rights reserved. No parts of this publication may be reproduced or transmitted, in any form or by any means, electronic or mechanical, including photocopying, recording on any information storage and retrieval system, without prior permission in writing from the publisher.

The right of Cliff Moiser to be identified as the author of this work has been asserted by him in accordance with the Copyright, Designs and Patents Act 1988.

Published by Basset Publications, Plymouth

Printed in Great Britain by
Peter Howell & Co.,
The Printing Press, 21 Clare Place, Coxside,
Plymouth PL4 0JW

For Colleen, with Love

By the same author

Road Traffic Endorsements and Disqualifications
Practice and Procedure in Magistrates' Courts

Preface

I went back to Dewsbury in June 1994 for a few days, to check some street names and other detail, the first time for well over 40 years with enough time to walk and browse. It was inevitable that things were not as I remembered them and I was saddened by much; the sorry state of St. Mark's Church, the complete run down of the Co-op building in Northgate, the loss of the Scarboro' pub opposite the Town Hall, and the Empire Theatre. Crown Flatt rugby ground and the Majestic cinema gone for ever. But there was much that was heartening, the people in particular, chirpy as ever, and just some signs of economic recovery. There were good pints of ale in the Black Bull, the Market House and the Little Saddle, and elsewhere. Cow heel was on sale in the market.

I could not make up my mind about the so called clean-up by steam heating of some public and private buildings, the Town Hall in particular. I suppose it looks nice and clean, and yet . . . . . there was something about the buildings that was not quite right, they were too clean and I missed the mature blackened stone which was such a feature of yesteryear. I kept wondering if I was the only one who saw beauty in grime covered stone.

I have written as I remembered and checked where I could but I must have got some things wrong; a Christian name, a year, a street, and I can only hope any reader affected will forgive me such errors. My other hope is that many readers will enjoy this trip back in time as much as I did writing it, which was tremendous fun.

"Ikey" Fowler (his wife Greta did not even know he was called Ikey at school until I got in touch a couple of years back) was kind enough to read the proofs for me and further remind me of our youth.

Floreat Dewsburia.

Cliff Moiser
Plymouth
September 1994

Growing Up in the West Riding
1925 to 1946

Chapter 1

We grew up 'midst dark satanic mills in Dewsbury, I suppose, but I was not really conscious of them, and took them for what they were, a source of income, modest for those at the bottom of the social pile, and considerable for those higher up. Smoke belched from the chimneys at Savile Town, Ravensthorpe and in the bowl that was, and is, Dewsbury but once you were atop Leeds Road, Wakefield Road and Halifax Road we appeared clear of it all. The fogs were bad, I gather they still are, but they did not last long. No-one ever called it smog them. The only low lying bit, along the banks of the Calder towards Mirfield, brought longer spells of mist and fog, and indeed ice, but they were not for ever. Wormalds and Walkers (inaugurated in 1824, or slightly earlier) must have been one of the biggest woollen mill employers, with modest pay for the workers, but they were turning out high quality work in the shape of blankets, rugs and suchlike, with sales worldwide.

It wasn't all mills though; Avery's weighing scales were made at Ravensthorpe and the firm had a worldwide reputation for high quality; Siemens had a presence at Staincliffe, producing what today would be called high tech equipment, later of great importance in some war weapons. There was a factory near Batley Carr, Speights, that made glass eyes for humans and for dolls, itself a most unusual business, but very profitable. Some of the other big boys were James Austin and Sons (Dewsbury) Ltd., Iron and Steel Stockholders and Structural Engineers, established in 1850. W.R. Thompson & Co. Ltd. were builders' merchants in Railway Street, founded in about 1780. W. Hodgson & Sons Ltd. were timber merchants at Scarborough Saw Mills, Savile Town, and that firm was started in 1860, so none of these firms could be called fly-by-nights. There were many others of course.

I was born in Kimberley Street at Thornhill Lees in 1925, (gas lighting and outside lavatory), in a Dewsbury that had a population of 54,000 and stretched from Thornhill, to Chickenley, to Batley Carr, to Dewsbury Moor and Staincliffe. It was a county borough (Motto: *Deus noster refugium et virtus,* (God our refuge and strength) and had been since 1910, when it joined with Thornhill, Ravensthorpe and parts of Soothill, which meant it mostly controlled its own destiny in the shape of local government so there was a Borough Council, with Dewsbury councillors and their own officials, ranging from the Town Clerk, through the Borough Treasurer and on through the Borough Education Officer, the Borough Engineer and the Borough Medical Officer with even a Borough Librarian. The civil servants, "the Mandarins", had not then fed their political masters with words such as "Economy of Scale", the words of villains and blackguards I later concluded, which created the chaos of the Local Government Act 1972, and forced neat little efficient towns into unholy alliances with unwanted neighbours for so called metropolitan or non-metropolitan districts. That had been preceded by amalgamating, amongst other things, police forces which lead to today's amorphous mass of forty three police forces, usually so big that one hand does not know what the other hand is doing, and with results of crime detection, for example, that would have made the old Borough Force officers cry. Many other of today's police activities would have had the same effect.

My father was a policeman in the then Dewsbury Borough Police Force, joining after the first World War, in which he served for the last three years, escaping unharmed except for a bit of shrapnel which nicked the bottom of his nose. He could recite the names and numbers of the entire police force, 1 to 60, led by the indomitable F.E. Pritchard, who always signed documents and letters in green ink, and why not, it was different.

My father was the village bobby at Thornhill Lees and my mother, a Halifax lass from a large family of nine, later opined that he thought, as pub licensing hours ended at 10 pm, the entire population of Thornhill Lees should be abed and asleep by 10,30 pm, but I do not think they were. He held strong views against the employment of women police officers, as most of the force then did, but Dewsbury was in the van in female appointments. There were certainly two in 1946, and I rather fancied (putting it mildly) Edna French, the junior of the two and very attractive. She achieved fame when, in civilian clothes, she was offered some illegal clothing coupons near the market. Without more ado, she clasped the villain, for such he was, to her bosom (something she never did for me) and screamed at the top of her voice until help arrived, as it did within seconds in those days. I would have given the bounder six months, partly because he had been close to her bosom, but he was only fined. I took her out to lunch a couple of times, but it soon petered out. She later became a Liberal councillor and stood as a Liberal Parliamentary candidate in Dewsbury, so it might be that even at the earlier time I suspected this minor blemish in her early education. I was never able to tell my father I had taken her out to lunch, or I might have been taken out of the Will. Bad behaviour in those days did sometimes lead to threats to disinherit, even if there was not much, if anything, to inherit. More than once I can recall that the Cats and Dogs Home would benefit considerably if my bad behaviour persisted.

The Dewsbury Borough Police Force also mostly ran the fire brigade in those days, and many of the policemen were also part time firemen. The entire police force was proficient in first aid and probably 80% held the St. John's Ambulance badge. But it took a war to create the Auxiliary Fire Brigade, full timers, later to become the National Fire Service and then later still to become decentralised under the county councils usually, for pay anyway, or still more ghastly amalgamations.

There were some advantages then in being the son of a policeman, not least the annual party for the children of policemen, held in the Town Hall and organised by some of that energetic police force, Sergeant Butler, Alan Reid, Maurice Crabtree, Barry Wilkinson and many others, with their wives. It was there I first became addicted to pork pies and sausage rolls (definitely Tom Green's or Walter Garside's) although there were vast quantities of sandwiches, cakes, ice cream and jellies to be consumed. More than one child was sick after such an event. The ice cream came from Caddy's, across the square, of which more later.

One or two scrapes were avoided by the words of the cautious Dewsbury youth, "Don't hit him, his father's a policeman." I often wonder if today the converse is true. I expect it is.

We moved, it was called flitting, from Thornhill Lees to Hartley Grove (electric lighting and inside lavatory and bathroom) in 1931 and our furniture was transferred by horse drawn van, still used more than motor vehicles. The two horses had a bit of difficulty in the last 100 yards, because it was uphill and the wheels slipped on loose ash, the ground covering of the Grove. My mother produced an apple or two for each horse which persuaded them to put extra effort into the job and we arrived in some style. The house backed on to some woods on one side, and Rock House Park on the other. Many's the time I was sent over the wall, through the park, to higher Batley Carr and its very superior quality fish and chips at 3½d—that is old pence—and next door, Verney Woods, for fat oozing cream slices at 2d. A meal fit for kings.

Thus it was that Carlton Road Juniors (Mixed) was my first real seat of learning, after only a few months at Thornhill Lees Infants via a short tram journey. The teaching staff at Carlton Road Juniors (Mixed) was led by those great educationalists (for the masses) J.E. Hanson, Norman Denham and Percy Rouse. We learned Geography by individual wall boxes indicating a map of England, Scotland and Wales which we prepared and slotted in behind the glass. These maps showed all the rivers and mountains, lakes and fells, and the whole lit up when the button was pressed, activated by a torch battery and torch bulb for which the fittings were provided. This was novel, to say the least, in those far off days but I can still remember most of the English rivers, from north to south down the east coast of England. Arithmetic was a bit more demanding, but we did, eventually, get to the proverbial bath which filled at the rate of two gallons a minute with both taps on, one gallon with only one tap. I got that bit but when it came to taking the plug out, so that water was lost at the rate of three gallons in four minutes, it all got a bit beyond me, and indeed most of us.

One highlight was a marvellous day in about 1933 by coach to Port Sunlight, on Merseyside, to view the manufacture of soap and other cosmetics. We got a free bar of soap and a free lunch, but Kenneth Lockwood says (in 1994 mind you) that he gave me his rice pudding as he didn't like it, and I ate two lots: I am unable to deny it.

With a natural cunning that I did not know I had, I escaped all duties such as milk monitor, and continued to do so throughout my formative years. There was a health clinic with free services to children, dental and medical, across Halifax Road and I was given the task of booking in that morning's clients one day. I know the nurse in charge was very pretty (she stayed there years) but the problem was I could hardly write as I was only 7 years old at the time. I did my scratching best with pen and blotchy ink, and even knew the difference between Derek and Derrick, but I could not have succeeded as I was never asked again. That clinic spent some time on teeth, but was also involved most of the time in examining heads—to seek and destroy small living creatures in the hair, called "nits". The avoidance procedure was to obey the family instruction not to wear anybody else's cap.

I was alongside children whose families really were poor, and who did not have boots or shoes, hence the charity "Boots for the Bairns" in being at the time. "Fatty" (Len) Sykes never had any boots and the best he ever achieved was plimsolls (pumps) both with holes at the toes and handed down from older brothers. He had no socks either, no coat, and no cap—he couldn't be blamed for passing on "nits"—but always pullovers with never less than two holes in them, also hand-me-downs. One or two of my co-learners wore clogs, which stopped "knock knees" according to the gossip. "Fatty" Sykes and I had a fight once, when we were eight or so, and I came out on top easily, because I was bigger. As I held him pinned to the ground I was encouraged by the many onlookers to bash his head into the concrete playground, but I couldn't do that. In fact we became friends after the fight which is often the way. The only thing that he ever owned, to my knowledge, was a pet rabbit, white at the front and black at the rear end.

We were in Rock House Park one day, "Fatty" with his rabbit, out for an airing, and me with my dog Raque, when suddenly apropos nothing at all, the dog went for the rabbit with which, until then he had had a reasonable if distant relationship. Luckily "Fatty" grabbed the rabbit and I grabbed the dog and we stopped a catastrophe, at the same time enriching our friendship through the shared danger. The last time I saw "Fatty" Sykes was on the platform of the railway station then opposite the Talk of the Town, at the bottom end of the market, in Crackenedge Lane. He was in naval uniform, but worse, with an armed escort of two naval provosts, obviously being taken back to his ship or other naval establishment. I was quite upset at the sight, we had been good friends, and I never even got the chance to have a kindly word, or offer him a cigarette, as his train came in, and that was the last I ever saw of him. Later, I suspected what I saw was a dreadful navy mistake (they did make them) because Fatty was not that sort of lad, but I never found out if it was or not. He had lived, with his large family, in pretty rough basement accommodation lower down Hartley Street, towards the mill at the bottom. In Hartley Grove, tradesmen called, the milkman twice a day, to ladle out milk into the customers' own jugs, but gossip had it they would never call on the poor families, as cash was not forthcoming. There was an abattoir at the bottom of Hartley Street, and it was natural for boys to look through the gap where the gates did not quite meet. They mostly slaughtered sheep, and I viewed it all through the gap. I only looked once and that was enough for me. I never looked again after that once.

The father of the Long twins of Hartley Grove was the manager of the mill at the bottom and we were allowed in to view the works. There were large drying tubs and we got in, to be pushed around for a free ride. All was well until Mr Long switched on the electric power one day, and the tubs shot round leaving us sick and dizzy for hours, after only one minute spinning. Never again for that, either.

I doubt my parents were God fearing citizens, although my father's family were Wet Wesleyans, entitling them to drink after chapel on Sundays. My mother's mother just forgot to have my mother christened at all, and it was not until about 1982, when she was turned 84, that she was christened in Plymouth. But from Hartley Grove I was sent to St, Mark's Church, in Halifax Road, some four hundred yards away, albeit uphill. It was there or the Parish Church (now Dewsbury Minster) which I declined on the grounds of distance. It would have made no difference to me even if I had known that Patrick Brontë, the father of Charlotte, Emily and Co., was the curate there about 1810. But I was impressed by the "Devil's Knell". It was and is a custom whereby on Christmas Eve, there was one stroke of the church bell for every year since the birth of Christ, said to keep the devil and evil away for the next year, but it's true origin was lost in history.

My family, especially my father, was quite superstitious and did not like the number 13, nor would they ever walk under ladders. The new moon had never to be seen through glass, and when you did see it you had to turn over any loose change in your pocket. I never saw it happen, but I was told boots and shoes were not to be placed on any table, as unemployment would automatically follow. Knives, even being prepared for washing up, must never be crossed or dire consequences would follow. These superstitions were not uncommon in local families, and there were many more, of which the Devil's Knell at the Parish church was just another example.

The setting out drill at St Marks was attendance on Sundays three times, morning service, Sunday school, and evensong, until I rebelled a bit, but only a bit. It paid to get just over fifty per cent attendance at Sunday school and the choir, to which I gravitated quite quickly, under the guidance of Ward Kemp a brilliant musician and choirmaster, later Maurice Lister. This was because of the annual Day-out 'bus trips for choir and Sunday school, and pay for the choir at two shillings a quarter, with the same fee for weddings and funerals, a couple or more a year. The choir trip, a one coach job, supplied by the Yorkshire Heavy Woollen District Transport Company, mostly made Bridlington, Scarborough or Filey. Peasholm Park in Scarborough was the scene of many a dashing encounter as we rode rented bicycles around the concrete area in mock racing. We took boats on the lake there, paddle boats for the younger and rowing boats for the older as we all mastered the art of the oars. The object of any boating was to be at the furthest end of the lake when the hour, or half hour, was up and the dreaded words "Come in number 10" were echoed across the water. You could get an extra 2 or 3 minutes if you were at the far end. The boating on the lake was popular because such opportunities were limited at home. There was boating on the lake at Crow Nest Park, and Boat Sam's at Ravensthorpe, on the Calder, alas considerably polluted by mill effluent. There were still boats as far down as Savile bridge occasionally but it silted up there most of the time.

The climax of the day out was the stop half way back to base for fish and chips, eaten in the coach. No one ever went without as even the spendthrift, with two or more rides on the bicycles and two or more boating trips plus candy floss and ice creams, had a penny given to them for chips, by the caring supervisors who were mostly adult members of the choir.

The Sunday school trips tended to be a bit more cultural with Fountains Abbey or Castle Howard high on the list. This was a three coach job, A, B and C, because the Sunday school attracted a larger number than the choir and parents were sometimes allowed to accompany their offspring, which was a bit inhibiting I thought.

A modest highlight came when, on an open stretch of road, coach B passed coach A, and then a bit later coach C passed coaches A and B. These were accompanied by much cheering in the overtaking coaches, and boos and catcalls from the overtaken. Quite unchurchlike some of it, but the parents inhibited a bit, as I said.

If there had been a clash between keeping the choir going, or Sunday School, the choir would have won hands down for me.

The Rev. Maughan M.A. was the vicar in charge all my time there, and his name was printed in gold on the church notice board facing Halifax Road. He lived in the vicarage next door, a veritable mansion with extensive grounds of lawns, shrubs and trees. The annual garden parties were held there, for adults actually, but I managed to get myself into two or three over the years. I did myself no harm when I devised a money making scheme, approved by the Rev. Maughan, by buying a fair old quantity of chocolate bars, Aero and the like, from the Talk of the Town, at 3½d for two, and selling them to the garden party attenders at 2½d a bar, the going rate. In fact the Rev. Maughan financed the original cash outlay at a couple of pounds or more, so taken was he by my business instinct. We obviously swelled the church profits to the tune of a pound or two, but I doubt now the church needed it. Surrounded as the church was by the inhabitants of Oxford Road and West Park Street, affluent areas in my eyes, the church was doing all right. It was at those garden parties I first became aware of the delights of cucumber sandwiches, made with wafer thin white or brown bread, butter and not that margarine rubbish, and importantly with the edges cut off. My gourmet tastes were being formulated.

For all that, the Rev. Maughan was a bit vague about how some of his flock lived, and we choir boys were gratified one day when he appeared in the vestry after evensong and offered us free tickets for a film show at the Playhouse Cinema, the latest and newest in town, and also a bag of sweets. We all accepted with alacrity, and came the day which we all thought went well. But horror, horror, a week later the *Dewsbury Reporter* carried the story, on the front page, that the poor children of the town had been treated to a free film show and given a bag of sweets and an orange by a local charity. What caused the real havoc was a photograph of the poor children, with St. Marks' choirboys in a prominent position in the front row, clutching the bag of sweets and that bloody orange. The choirboy parents of Oxford Road and West Park Street did not take kindly to this, nor did my parents. The choirboys were not allowed to know what happened, well I wasn't, but I knew that things were said, and it would not have surprised me if the affair got to the notice of the Parochial Church Council, or even the Bishop. But in time it all died down, as these things do. I only saw the Rev Maughan rattled once, and that was when the choirmen (not boys) once talked overmuch and overloud during his sermon. He turned round in the pulpit, mid sentence, and threatened to leave it forthwith unless they packed it in. They stopped, sharpish, and I was able to continue sucking my mint imperial, or was it my aniseed ball, then retailing at ten for ½d. The Rev Maughan's sermons consistently lasted twenty minutes, give or take a minute either way, and he would have been nowhere in the Great Sermon Handicap Stakes, created for Bertie Wooster and Steggles by P.G. Wodehouse; unless indeed he got fifteen or twenty minutes start in the handicap. He was so consistent on time that we choirboys ceased to bet on the length of the sermon.

I was in church the day war was declared in 1939, so 3rd September must have been a Sunday. We all got there to hear the Rev. Maughan indicate that the Prime Minister would make an important announcement at 11 am and the service was cancelled, the only time I can ever remember that happening. I set off home, a couple of miles away by then, but actually heard that no answer had been received to the British ultimatum and therefore we were at war with Germany, on the radio—it was called wireless then—in the home of Sid Redhead, a fellow chorister, in a little terrace house, first left up Willans Road where it left Halifax Road. I doubt we children understood the impact all this was to have on our lives, but we soon found out, of course. Our parents seemed to know only too well. I was confirmed not at St Marks, but at Dewsbury Moor Church in May 1941, by the Bishop of Pontefract.

But before all this, in the mid to late thirties, I thought, and still think, that life was rich. There were five cinemas, and this was the day of the feature film, a B movie, often a cowboy saga, Pathe News and a feature of forthcoming attractions. All for 2d or at the worst 4d, the half price for children figures. The Playhouse, which opened in 1931, seemed to be the most modern, at the lower end of the market at Crackenedge Lane, and now Mecca Bingo—oh dear! The Regal was opposite the Town Hall, at the end of the market place, the Pioneers was in the Co-operative building, below the bottom of Halifax Road, the Tudor, formerly the Theatre Royal, was down a dark alley off Bradford Road, near the cut or beck which I think was actually part of a canal, and the Majestic (it had been the Trinity Congregational church) was up a great flight of steps, opposite the corner of the Co-op building (the cake and bun department next to the tobacconist) where it joined Wellington Road.

Both the Regal and the Playhouse had Wurlitzer organs, with resident organists, to play in the intervals between films. It was a matter of wonder how those mighty organs rose from the bowels of the earth, in front of the screen, all aglow with coloured lights. The music started from the bowels when all the lights came on, much to the dismay sometimes of the back row, downstairs, where courting couples had to undergo a quick disentanglement. The back row had seats for two, the rest of the house being singles. Red Sails in the Sunset was popular music on the organ as was one about being down Mexico way. Organ time was also ice cream time when young ladies appeared each with a tray of various ices in tubs with flat wooden spoons, but never any cornets alas.

My mother favoured the Pioneers (no dividend on entrance fees though) where afternoon tea could be provided during the interval, or during the film, for 9d, to be eaten in your cinema seat from a tray. I think you could only have tea if you were at the back in the one shilling seats, and the offer did not apply to the sixpennies and the ninepennies, at the front. It was a good tea, ham or cucumber sandwiches, a scone well buttered, a sticky bun, with which I always had difficulty, and a pot, not a cup, of tea. My father occasionally joined my mother at the cinema, but was eventually banned by her because, as the National Anthem was played at the end of a performance, as good a way as any of saying it was all over, there was a mad dash for the exits, but my father insisted on standing fast, at attention, until the last note died away, even the longer version which lasted two or three minutes. The final straw for my mother was in the early days of the war, when my father would insist on clapping his hands loudly every time Winston Churchill appeared on screen, mostly in the News bit. Other people then joined in but only after looking to see who started it.

The Majestic was known as the flea pit, and it was rumoured that entry could be gained by two jam jars but I never saw that happen. There were matinees for 1d, at the half price children rate. Front two rows only for that and that was where trouble sometimes erupted. The Majestic projector seemed a bit more unreliable than most, and when it broke down there was much booing and shouting from the louts at the front. Fighting was known to occur. Alas, those to the rear also joined in and it was bedlam. The manager, and he was a bit deaf which didn't help, would then appear centre stage from the wings, and threaten to knock heads together if the noise did not stop. No notice was ever taken of this warning, nor when one or two heads were actually knocked together. What brought peace was (a) the re-start of the projector usually at a point in the film quite different to the break-down point or (b) when the manager threatened to eject the noisiest, especially when he actually carried out the threat once or twice. The patrons knew that was the end, and there was no chance of getting the 1d or 2d entrance fee back, or the jam jars, if indeed they were accepted.

The films came in reels, and it was known for the last reel to be shown first, so you got the ending of the film before the beginning. When it dawned on the paying customers what had happened, and it was not always apparent quickly, the catcalls and booing started but were quelled again as at (a) and (b) above.

The manager of the Majestic cinema, Ernest Dixon, was a friend of my father's and I had a free ticket there for several years, upstairs in the balcony too. I also got cigarettes there when they became scarce a year or so into the war; the cinemas got a ration of cigarettes as shops, provided they had supplied them previously. Most did and cinemas varied considerably in the density of the blue fug which hung over all the emporia during the movies, depending on the efficacy of the scent sprays used. It was unthinkable to ban smoking in there, or even have no smoking areas, and every seat back carried a brass ashtray. The seat backs today probably carry a government health warning, but I wouldn't know as I never go. It's their loss.

Gangster films were much in vogue at this time, as films were coming through showing the effects of prohibition in the United States. "Scarface" was one such and the manager of the Majestic, Mr. Dixon, who really was enterprising considering his antiquated equipment, produced personally on stage, at a suitable moment after the film a real live hoodlum, on a visit from America, who had been "taken for a ride" by hoodlums of the enemy gang, shot and left for dead, but he recovered miraculously to tell the tale. He actually showed the bullet marks on his body. We were all terribly impressed by this and George Raft and James Cagney were never the same again after that.

Laurel and Hardy were in their heyday with Harold Loyd, Buster Keaton and Wheeler and Wolsely all good comedy value. We were not, as children, much into the Love stories, but we could stand Johnny Weissmuller as Tarzan, and Sonja Henie as an ice skating beauty. My own preference was for British films and I saw Will Hay with Graham Moffatt and Moore Marriott in "Oh, Mr Porter" not less than twelve times. And all, but all, their other films, with "Ask a Policeman" in the top ten. George Formby, Gracie Fields, and even Len Harvey, the British heavyweight boxing champion, in films were compulsive viewing and it was a good night out to see a British comedy, an American cowboy (with Indians, must have Indians) B movie, even with Ronald Reagan, although Tom Mix or Gene Autry were better, the News and an ice cream half way through. A total cost of some 6d, and it could be topped up, if funds allowed, with chips, if not fish and chips, on the way home. At this stage of the game, girls did not come into it, as all they would have done was double the cost, and for what purpose some of us asked ourselves, being naive and with the innocence of youth. But we saw what our elders were doing, especially in the back row.

Live theatre was a different ball game. This was centred on the Empire Theatre, built in 1909, just below the then Post Office at the bottom of Leeds Road, and opposite the side of the Town Hall. That is not to say amateur theatricals did not take place and I appeared modestly as an elf in a production of Iolanthe by the St Mark's Players, staged in the Sunday School Hall, at the back of St Mark's Church. My mother had the photograph of the entire cast with Gladys Wilkinson as a Princess. All I remember, being literally stitched into the green elf costume which covered me all over, was pulling out the stitches to get to the lavatory (the words toilet, loo, comfort station or wash-room were not then used), an event which had not been foreseen. We had it on high authority that our elfish antics were carried out well. I fancied one of the fairies actually, but now forget which.

Mr Sterry was the manager and in charge of the Empire Theatre for years, and good quality stuff it was too, covering the whole theatre spectrum. Anne Ziegler and Webster Booth sang, but I liked the music hall type of show best, and the favourites in comedy, stand up comedians, were Stainless Stephen, Frank Randle, Dickie Henderson (senior), Mr Muddlecombe J.P., Sandy Powell ("Can you hear me, Mother?") and Albert Modley. Albert Modley liked a pint or two when he was appearing at the Empire and my father was his drinking companion on quite a few occasions. Years later I met the late Dickie Henderson (junior) when he stayed at the rather posh hotel where I was conferencing and we reminisced about the old music hall days of his father. Dickie (junior) remembered Dewsbury well, and as a child he used to accompany his parents when they were on tour. I think he said they stayed at the Scarboro' or the Black Bull, which was convenient if nothing else and vastly superior to the usual actors' landladies, in digs. Phyllis Dixie, the stripper appeared, but I was not allowed anywhere near, nor allowed to look at the advertisement boards showing forthcoming attractions. My eyes were shielded. After WW2 my future wife and I had virtually the same two seats for months, if not years, on Saturday nights when the local Repertory company performed, augmented by one or two stars or future stars in leading roles each week. Cicely Courtnedge and Jack Hulbert one week, followed by Anthony Newley, Barbara Murray and Lana Morris, followed in turn by Mai Zetterling and many more of similar standing.

Pantomime ran from December to about February, which was all it would stand, and Dewsbury could not compete with Leeds where the panto often ran through to April or beyond. But I think the management knew what it was doing and there was more than one circus there on stage. I saw my first lions and tigers there and at one stage I was so taken by it all I considered a career as a lion tamer, but nothing came of it. I did practice in front of a mirror with a home made whip in my right hand, and a bamboo chair, legs pointing away, in my left. My mother said I damaged the chair, and my dog would not be persuaded to act the lion/tiger part. He shot off and was not seen for hours.

After WW2 the Batley Variety Club took the lead with Rock Bands, Shirley Bassey, Louis Armstrong and big name comedians and so on, in premises on Bradford Road just outside the Borough boundary. Those premises had been a skating rink and then it held boxing bouts, wrestling when things got bad, but the boxing was good. The Irishmen Pat and Mick Igo, who lived near "Fatty" Sykes, performed there and were good fighters. They beat the living daylights out of challengers (and each other) for £5 a night—up to six rounds too. Dewsbury Feast always started in the last week of July and the fairground came to town, at the far end of Rishworth Street, on railway property. It was all there, and I favoured brandy snap, rolled into a finger. Candy floss was reasonably priced as was the ice cream, needed because the whole affair was on cinder tracks throwing up dust by the ton. We breathed it in and didn't care. I managed more than one woolly toy on the shooting range, and dozens of goldfish in bowls, even though we knew the sights on the rifles had been "tampered with". "Dodgem" cars and the "Big Dipper" were available at 3d a go.

The boxing booths were in their heyday too, and all fairs had them. It was said a hungry fighter was a good fighter, and many a British champion started in the fairground boxing booths. The resident heavy threw out the challenge to anyone in the audience to last three two minute rounds with him and win £5. The Igo brothers were always on hand to accept the challenge from the audience and mostly lasted three rounds to collect £5, and nobbins (money in the shape of coins thrown into the ring by the audience following a good performance) worth maybe another £5. Sometimes a member of the audience accepted the challenge spontaneously, and not as a plant like the Igos, but they often did not fare so well in lasting three rounds; on the other hand I saw a local beat the resident heavy who, to my knowledge had already had two or three previous bouts that day. I had the feeling there was not much medical assistance about, other than the magic sponge and smelling salts. The timekeeping was a bit shaky too, with a bout going well over two minutes if the resident heavy was doing well, but decidedly under two minutes if the resident heavy was getting walloped and coming off worst. It cost a shilling for adults to get in, for two three round contests, and was thought to be good value. I once got in free, by crawling under the canvas marquee, at the back, but I can recall paying 3d when in funds.

The swimming baths, opened as far back as 1896, and the library were next to each other in Wellington Road, at the Ravensthorpe end, but John Major's classless society had not arrived then as now. There were two swimming pools, first class and second class, and I only made the first class once and that by mistake. The only difference was that the first class water was cleaner and the changing cabins around the pool, were a bit more spacious. I learned to swim and dive in the second class pool and later got free swimming when visiting with school parties.

Exotica was further provided by Turkish, Russian, Vapour and Zotofoam Baths; alas they were all beyond my price range, at 6d a time.

Culture was provided with books from the library which included a very good children's section. We joined at no cost but it was expensive to keep a book over 14 days, at 1d a week. Woe betide the youngster who lost his "library ticket" a priceless possession, as the rule of "no ticket, no book" was rigorously enforced. Silence was enforced by a stream of attractive young ladies who sported perfume, maybe the Chanel No. 5 of today. It was a good place to be and to linger, as the perfume did. Not that our reading was confined to *Robinson Crusoe*, *Just William* (Brown) and *Huckleberry Finn*, far from it: the comics in great demand pre-war were *Adventure*, *Hotspur*, *Wizard*, *Rover*, *Magnet* and *Film Fun*. I never rated *Film Fun* for some reason, and if I had a preference it was for *Adventure*, which seemed to provide more free gifts with its 2d weekly issues than the others. One such was a glider; in fact two bits of balsa wood which fitted together with a piece of elastic, but it did go. It flew the maximum air miles in Rock House Park, but came to an ignominious end when a friend trod on it. Rock House Park, because it rose steeply towards Batley Carr (Upper) was a good place for flying kites too, and I performed there, with others, until this time a friend sat on mine in a careless moment. The real place for kite flying though was the top of Pildacre Hill, in Ossett, but overlooking Chickenley. People did not sit on your kite there, simply because no one else was there.

Our family newspaper reading was conservative. The *Reporter* was a prime purchase on Saturdays, and if it was not available (very rare) then the *District News* was taken. Most evenings we read the *Yorkshire Evening Post* but never the *Yorkshire Evening News* which seemed taboo. Newspaper vendors came round the streets shouting, and there was no need to order from any newspaper shop. I remember taking an interest in Con Gordon of the *Evening Post* when he started a series called "Courts Day by Day", most hilarious accounts of the goings on in the lower courts. It took the mickey but was no worse for it. The so called 'quality' papers never darkened our doorstep, as the saying went, and it was well post war before I read the *Times* or the *Telegraph* daily. Just occasionally I might see the *Yorkshire (Morning) Post* but I never became an addict. The *Yorkshire Observer* also had a low family profile.

Because Dewsbury is a comparatively small town, and I mostly lived within a mile or two of the town centre, my mode of transport was on foot, certainly until the advent of bicycle number 1 which arrived when I was about 11 years of age. Keith Waterhouse in his book *City Lights*, relates how he wandered around Leeds on foot, and enjoyed staring at all that City had to offer to a child growing up there. My recollection is that there never was any time to stand and stare, there was too much to do, and it was a quick look and onwards. The tram ride, later the bus ride from 1935, from Dewsbury to Ossett always fascinated me. Up Wakefield Road, through the cutting as it was called, on past Earlsheaton Park on the right, and then down past Bywell Road, past the cemetery and into the dip which was taken at breakneck speed. One bus actually rolled over there pre-war, with many casualties but luckily no deaths There was Shaw Cross pit on the left as you went up the other side with horrible slag heaps gradually getting nearer and nearer to the

Wakefield Road. It is all green grass now but it was a bit rough then. On to Chickenley and turn right into Ossett, where the tram came to a grinding halt near the Town Hall. Sitting upstairs on the tram (pre 1935) I found the vista enthralling, and it was heaven sitting in the open air bit, front and rear, where the thrill of it all was at its highest. Visiting Ossett gave me the impression of being well travelled and knowing quite a bit of the outside world.

I could never quite fully understand the LMS/LNER railway system serving Dewsbury, which is a pity as I am now into Hornby clockwork trains in my later years. There were three railway stations, one at the top of Wellington Road, (LMS I think) and still there, one at the bottom of the market in Crackenedge Lane, (where I last saw "Fatty" Sykes) opposite the Talk of the Town, (methinks LNER—the gates still there) and one bang outside the Town Hall, demolished about 1931 or 1932 and turned into air raid shelters with a grass top later. I knew the Town Hall one ran trains to Thornhill, but beyond that I was a bit lost, although London St Pancras rings a bell. In fact it was the Yorkshire and Lancashire Railway Company, and there is a large map showing this exactly, on the wall in the lounge of the Market House Inn, at the bottom of Daisy Hill. It took holiday makers to Blackpool and the West Coast. The one by the bottom of the market must have led to the sea, somewhere, or "Fatty" Sykes in naval uniform would not have been there; I suspect it went south via Wakefield. I know the monthly return fare, Dewsbury to London, 3rd Class, was thirty-two shillings. The 2nd Class had disappeared.

The Wellington Road railway I do know led to adventure, and also brought in the fish from Hull and Grimsby. It led to those resorts in another county, Blackpool, Morecambe and Southport, veritable fleshpots. You could get to those on day trips, much favoured by my mother, for three shillings and six pence adult, one shilling and nine pence child, liberally construed. The half day trips were even cheaper. My mother insisted we did this regularly, without father who had been banned again, maybe for having a couple of pints in Blackpool; that in itself was not a problem, but it was when the train back (most of them) had no corridor and hence no access to a lavatory. Having said that, I suspect she made a mountain out of a molehill, because kindly, understanding guards kept the train waiting a minute or two at intermediate stations for passengers to make hurried journeys to the station lavatory to deal with the calls of nature, albeit aided and abetted by Tetley's (or even Webster's) bitter.

Blackpool Tower was a fine sight to us children, and it was essential to see and hear Reg Dixon at the Tower organ. He also played his organ music over the radio, from the Tower, for BBC, but was said to have gone a bit 'eccentric' at the end. However, once having seen it and getting past the sand castle stage, the amusement arcades beckoned. I always fancied myself on the cranes, at 1d a go. Once activated the crane moved by lever right or left, and up and down for a short period, and the object was to get the crane grab to pick up a gold wristlet watch (it said it was gold) or a bejewelled ring (it said it was a jewel) set amongst Bassett liquorice allsorts. I won enormous quantities of liquorice allsorts but never the watch or ring. Nobody else won them either as far as I could see, as even if the grab picked up the goodies it managed to drop them just before the crane grab was about to unload down the chute.

There was only one "amusement" arcade in Dewsbury, in Foundry Street, at the top end of the market, and it had the usual array of 1d in the slot fruit machines. It also had two other attractions, firstly the daughter of the proprietor, who, although quite pale faced and blond, was attractive and on duty changing money and so on sometimes. She sat on a pedestal in the middle, where I would have put her anyway. On these occasions I would amble in to chat her up and see psychology practised at first hand, my first introduction to it, and which I quickly saw through. If you handed in a one shilling piece, you should get twelve 1d coins back; not here, you were actually given fourteen on the basis you would spend it all anyway. Some of us left with a 2d or 4d profit. It really was the so modest fore-runner of the present day gaming casino where all the booze and smoked salmon sandwiches are "free"; or the Moscow casino where half a dozen of my rugby team, playing there a year or two back, were actually given three hundred dollars just to stay and gamble a little more.

Chapter 2

St Annes-on-Sea had the honour of receiving the Moiser family for a minimum of two weeks in the summer holidays. We did that year after year without thought of going anywhere else. I was rarely consulted. We could not afford hotels, nor the usual idea of a boarding house. We stayed with the Timms in their house about a mile back from the sea front, and Mrs Timms prepared the food for three meals a day that my mother bought. It was still good fun and we were lucky in the sense that many people had no holiday at all at the seaside. I saw my first Walls tricycle "Stop Me and Buy One" in St Annes, and became very partial to, I suppose, coloured iced water shaped like Toblerone, at ½d a shot, ice cream being then beyond my range. My teeth have never recovered.

In later life I have often been accused of over-eating, being a glutton, and charitably, a gourmet. I am none of those, of course, but I have to say food has loomed large in my life, just as staring loomed large for Keith Waterhouse. My mother excused my normally good appetite, no more than that, on the grounds that I was "a big lad". It was a mark of approval in our circles if mother "kept a good table". I like to think I was brought up "proper", and I knew at an early age not to eat peas off a knife. To take soup from the far side of the plate, although to this day I take it from the front, being perverse, and leave my knife and fork at 45 degrees across the plate when finished. We were civilised to the extent that at home we ate Yorkshire Pudding as a separate course, either with gravy to start with, or with Golden Syrup or treacle after the main course, inevitably meat. None of this Yorkshire Pudding came in little round circles either, it was cooked in a dish about one foot square and cut into four, and four only so you got a fair whack, some six inches by six inches or more. And there were seconds if need be. How my mother did that, and sometimes she baked her own bread in her own bread tins, I will never know because most of my childhood she cooked on an open coal fire and a front grate, with a side oven under which the burning coals could be pushed. Topped up by an old-fashioned gas ring, that's all she had.

Tripe, of course, was a staple diet but we patronised butchers many and varied for it, no one seller having a monopoly. Cow heel was plentiful and my favourite, but I have not had a touch of it since I left Dewsbury. Tripe and onions, funnily enough, did not feature large in my diet. Black pudding, polony and haslet were for high tea, but never fried black pudding. All pork products came from Tom Green, later Walter Garside and "Porky" Cross, (still in business in the covered market) and all produced small individual pork pies that were hot, with the gravy oozing out from a little hole in the top of the crust. I have never seen one of those for twenty years or more either.

We did not get much into restaurants those days, but I knew the Playhouse was for the hoi poloi, with Hagenbachs and Dempster Lister up amongst the leaders, and the Co-op giving value for money as always. My own favourite was Bailey's, next door to Woolworths and up the stairs, and still there. At times of family crisis I ate there and was always able to charge it to my father, an advantage not shared by many. There was a jolly good blow out for one shilling and three pence, three courses, and my day was made if served by the attractive waitress with red hair, Phyllis Bailey, no less, whose daughter still works there. I seemed to get bigger helpings when she was on duty, and it was there I perfected my "little boy lost" demeanour, later developed with age into my "helpless look" in stores where the assistants were female. The older you get the more do most female shop assistants respond to it and I have no sympathy with those who today bemoan lack of attention in shops as the assistants paint their nails or gossip about last night's adventure with the latest boyfriend. They just do not play it right. In 1994 the Yorkshire pudding and gravy at Bailey's tasted just as good as in 1934.

A bit more down market and approaching my level was a pub/cafe at the top of Daisy Hill, on the left before you turn right to Wellington Road and the library. Every day except Sunday it had a giant meat and potato pie on a heater but visible from the street through its window. It must have been two feet by two feet, always part sold and never whole, but with steam floating from it. Countless times, whenever passing in fact, I stood, glued to the window a bit like the Bisto Kid, and ogled it. It was 2d a time, with bread, but I never actually got in there, ever, because I never had 2d at the right time. Inside were trestle tables and bench seats, but there was some class because the tables had oilcloth table "cloths", and mustard was provided. How I ached for that pie, but even with my "little boy lost" look I never got asked in for a free portion—the entire place was staffed by men, obviously with hard hearts.

Later on, when I was about 13, I became a patron of the Criterion, a wooden shack affair at the bottom of Halifax Road, where it joins Willans Road, and opposite t'mill which was government offices, and the new Safeway. The speciality of the house was peas, green or black, served in gravy with bread for ½d. But if you could afford 1d you got a bigger helping and also a Woodbine cigarette and a match. I mostly raised 1d, but you had to accept that at those prices you could not expect an oilcloth table "cloth" at the trestle tables, which were uncovered. I think the seating capacity was about 14, but the proprietor managed to get 20 in on occasions. There was a time when certain Headmasters thought the place a corrupting influence and the Woodbine did it, not the peas; so much so that there was talk of the place being banned and I think it was to one or two schools. Whatever they did, they got it wrong because all that did was increase the number of customers and I have seen 24 in there, shortly after school ended at 4pm. I saw power and privilege at work there, although I did

not realise it at the time, because a privileged clientele
was created, of which I happened to be one, and we got
preference for entry against newcomers. I only hope the
Elders of the Dewsbury Church built on the site are aware
of the sheer historic value of what they bought.

Any discussion about restaurants and food leads
naturally to Dewsbury shopping. The market was always
highly thought of in towns around us, and people came
from miles away for the weekly shopping. All I know is
it was much more fun than a present day supermarket.
Market days found the two parts of the market in full
swing, the covered market and open market with its
stalls, hired by the day from the council. There was even
a Markets Department within the Borough Council, and
I found out it actually ran at a profit. Originally, the Duke
of Leeds had the right to all market tolls under a Feudal
tenure, but the Council bought him out. Food was in the
covered market with as many as fifteen to twenty
butchers. Farm produce was there aplenty and our fruit
was bought from Willie Hooper at the top end, facing
Foundry Street. Meat we got where it appeared best, and
there were knock-down prices as the closing hour of 9pm
approached on Fridays and Saturdays. We shopped 8pm
to 9pm when finances were low.

For some reason my parents were against frozen New
Zealand meat which I was told was for poorer families,
and we always had what was called "home killed" meat.
Similarly we were on locally produced butter and cheese.
Years and years later, when my family decided it was
violently opposed to being part of Europe, nothing

produced in Europe was permitted in the home, and New Zealand butter was mandatory. Alas, all too late for New Zealand which had to find other markets after Britain joined the European Comedy, and my parents had to take some of the blame, certainly for the meat position. We ate none but Killingbecks eggs which were laid by contented free range hens living at Thornhill. To some extent I think we were gastronomic snobs, if that is possible, but whatever we had was "noorishing" as Professor John Baldwin of Birmingham University said about our childhood when we discussed it. He was a Burnley lad and whilst not always accepting what comes out of Lancashire, he was about right on this one.

Groceries we always purchased at the local Co-op, and I can still remember our check number as 9658. This was crucial to our well-being as every purchase was logged and every quarter a dividend on sales was proclaimed, to be drawn in cash or, if you had a Co-op bank account, credited to that account. There was family excitement at dividend time and although ours was credited to the Co-op bank account, it was usually drawn out in cash within a few days, from the banking department in the Co-op building. Whether or not our dividends were spent on drink I do not know but it was a time of rejoicing and treats, even if only another day by rail to Blackpool.

One of the last of the real old fashioned stores was Spiking's, up Bond Street on the left and we used that occasionally. Bill Spiking ran it eventually, but his Uncle, who had served in WW1 with my father, before that. Wooden floor, a chair or two for the elderly to sit down 'midst the beautiful smell of ground coffee of the highest quality; hams hanging, whole cheeses and tea from the Universe.

The ice cream parlour though was Caddy's, and Caddy's alone, a complete monopoly. The parlour was situated opposite the Town Hall, but through a "ginnel", and next to Worfolks, the toy shop in Tithe Barn Street. Some affluence with plush seats in the eating area. The owners were the Cadiamatri (I think spelled like that) brothers who lived in Bywell Road and were real Italians, with the know-how about ice cream that seems peculiar to Italy. For 2d you got a handled glass of ice cream, full to the brim with a wafer stuck on the top to finish it off. A metal spoon was the implement supplied for eating and you were expected to retire to the parlour or lounge. Other more exotic ices were available but nothing over six pence for many years, and the exotica was merely coloured fruit juice poured on, or a couple of cherries, and not worth the extra I always thought. You could get a penny wafer but that did not entitle you to use the parlour and seemed very ordinary. It was unusual to see people eating ices in the street but I suppose they must have done.

Years later, in 1946, I got home from the Royal Marines and worked in the magistrates' court for George Ferguson, who was then the magistrates' clerk. I would have been articled to him on the way to becoming a solicitor, but for his untimely death. The office I used was next but one to that of the Chief Constable, F.E. Pritchard, no less, and he used to sit in a council

committee room, just across our corridor, which looked
out on the ginnel, which in turn was the entry to Caddy's.
I came across him there late one Friday and he invited
me to watch dozens of men entering the ginnel and
heading towards Caddy's (or Worfolks toy shop which
was unlikely). I thought Caddy's must be making a
fortune in ice cream sales, until Mr Pritchard told me
that he would have to do something, as a lot of wives
were writing to him, complaining that their husbands
were arriving home on Fridays with no money, having
gambled away their earnings at Caddy's. This was an
eye-opener for me, still naive, as I assumed they were
all buying ice cream. Sure enough warrants to search
were applied for a day or so later, and granted, which
led to a police raid on the place. There were dozens in
there, possibly a hundred, at the time of the raid, all
betting away the family wages allocated for groceries, at
various events, including blackjack, roulette and even
poker. All the participants were arrested and charged
with illegal gaming as it then was, with the Caddy
brothers and others charged with running the show. All
pleaded guilty eventually to the charges, and the minor
gamblers fined modest amounts, but the Caddy brothers
and other organisers had particularly heavy fines
imposed upon them, several thousand pounds in total,
the penalty for running a gambling den. The Caddy
brothers were really hard working members of Dewsbury
society, and very nice people to boot. Today they would
just get a gaming licence, which presumably would pay
for itself, and not risk inflation as this episode clearly
did when their ice cream went up in price; I always

assumed to pay the heavy fines. In those days half the
fines for gambling offences went to the Borough Council,
and the Borough Treasurer himself, A.E. Richardson,
honoured me with a call in my office to ascertain how I
was doing getting the fines in. It mattered to him, because
if everybody paid up and did not go to prison for default
in payment, it meant a saving of almost 1d on the council
rate poundage. I am pretty clear 95% of those fines were
collected eventually and the ratepayers benefited,
especially if they did not eat ice cream and thereby pay
the subsequent higher prices at Caddy's.

Cricket, which played a large part in my later life,
was centred on Savile Town, the one time home of
Dewsbury and Savile. It was a superb cricket field with
a good true wicket in the thirties. The Yorkshire county
side played there until about 1936, and I saw several
county games. The greats were there, Herbert Sutcliffe,
Wilfred Rhodes, Maurice Leyland, Frank Smailes, A.B.
Sellers, Hedley Verity, Bill Bowes and the rest, when
Yorkshire were in their best days, winning the county
championship year after year. I never knew why
Dewsbury lost the county fixtures, too young, but it could
not have been because of the wicket. Even after WW2
the dressing rooms provided accommodation for the
gentlemen and the players, both sides, but the stand and
pavilion were wearing a badly run-down look.

I have heard it said that the old Yorkshire county
cricket tale was enacted at Dewsbury, and certainly the
dressing room geography was right. I am pretty sure
Lancashire played there even though Headingley

obviously snaffled most games. Brian Sellers gathered his four gentlemen players together, ready to field, and passed the player's (professionals) dressing room door, where the seven pro's were expected to come out and tag on behind the gentlemen, on to the field of play. Sellers saw the professional fast bowler, not quite ready to take the field, but on his knees praying, and heard "Oh Lord, if it's thy Will that Lancashire win, they'll win; if it's thy Will that we win, we'll win. But Lord, if tha'll just keep out o' this one, we'll give 'em one heck of a thrashing today".

Opposite the main entrance, in Savile Road, was a small block of shops which were very convenient for snacks and I never saw snacks sold in the ground to spectators. Tom Green had a shop there for the popular pork pie, and next door was the shop that sold sweets and minerals. Most youngsters drank Tizer, but my gourmet tastes were even then evident and I was into Dandelion and Burdock. This was 1d a bottle, with ½d given back when you returned the bottle. Somehow I contrived mostly to buy one bottle, but take two back as bottles discarded by the affluent were not difficult to find.

At that entrance to the ground on the right was a field with a couple of horses in, grazing. They were the last of the police horses used by the Dewsbury Borough Police Force Mounted Section, and my father was one of the last to ride them. After he died I inherited his spurs which I later sent to West Yorkshire Police who put them in their museum to recall the days of mounted police in Dewsbury.

The Dewsbury Police Cricket Team played one or two games which I saw there and what a side it was. It was another example of so much talent being provided by a small force. George Meetham was as graceful an opening bat as you could find, with many a fifty to his name. Joe Burgin was a fast bowler of tremendous strength, as fast as Bill Bowes I would say, on his day. Wily left hand spinners came from Maurice Crabtree, and all those three would have made a county side of today's standards. I think two of them played for Yorkshire 2nd XI but even that turned on the consent of the Chief Constable, and it was not always forthcoming, duty coming first. To get three days off at one time for a game was asking the impossible. I played on that ground a few times before and after WW2. In the top right hand corner, near the pavilion, was the bowling green, crown of course, and one day I hit a glorious six, the ball landing bang in the middle of the bowling green. It was some hit. Old men appeared from the bowling green at its entrance from the ground, and as their arms were waving I thought they were congratulating me. Alas, when their words floated across to the middle I could hear they were not, indeed they were very angry and threatened me with violence if I did it again. I thought they were not very good sportsmen, none of the give and take spirit, which I thought bowlers of their age, none under 60, would have. Nor did I think that bowlers of that age even knew some of those words, let alone wish to use them. I never hit one into Savile Road which some of the county players managed although I never saw one do it. I once saw

Eddie Paynter, the Lancashire and England batsman, hit a six on the Ossett ground in an early wartime charity game. The ball was not recovered and it was said to have landed in a coal truck on a passing train and ended up at Worcester. The story was never confirmed to my satisfaction.

The nearest horse racing track was, and still is, Pontefract but I only went there once as a child, horse racing and gambling being near to corruption it was said. Pontefract must be the only race track in the world where a notice advised jockeys to take the last corner wide as the ground on the inside of the bend was liable to subsidence due to coal mining. I often wondered how many races were lost when the jockeys did go wide, and if any horse and jockey ever disappeared into the bowels of the earth on the bend, or into a disused pit. It was a far cry from Royal Ascot which I later attended as part of my work. Tommy Weston was the local jockey, from West town, and rode on occasions I believe, for Miss Dorothy Paget and the Aga Khan, winning several classics. The gossip amongst the intelligentsia was not to back his tips as they were most unreliable but I never had funds to test this theory.

The air of permanence we grew up with was reflected in the shops, quite apart from the market, which had a bewildering array of clothes. I had a "leisure" shirt with short sleeves, grey woollen material, bought from a market stall for one shilling about 1936. It was a favourite shirt and it had to be prised off me eventually around

1945, when it dropped to bits. I would still have been wearing it if it had been left to me. More formal clothing would come from "John's, the Hat and Shirt Boss" whose emporium was in Church Street, near the parish church, facing the solicitors, Messrs. Chadwick Son and Nicholson, and next to the Allotment Association. John, who had several other outlets in Lancashire, made periodic visits to Miss Ainsworth the manageress, and a friend of my mother, who would have assisted in the shop there but for restrictions on working for the wives of policemen, rigorously enforced. John had a motor car, with which he travelled from Lancashire, and I was privileged to be taken for a spin one day, about 1934, my first ride in a motor car. On the open road I saw the speedometer touch 55 miles per hour and that was living as the car was open topped on that occasion.

My mother's brother, Harry, sold tea wholesale in Halifax for Brooke Bond, and had the use of a Trojan van, used for Brooke Bond by the fleet. I went with him on his rounds in the Trojan several times, and it was just as exhilarating as a Morgan 3-wheeler.

Next door to John's was the Allotment Association which sold seeds and plants at very realistic prices; it was a non-profit making affair, and we used it often. On the present site, an agricultural shop, is a plaque commemorating its founding in 1917 by Mr Bowley and others.

Burtons, the Tailor of Taste, was in business in Corporation Street, but we patronised Jessops in the market place where Mr Stell was the manager in charge. I first heard the words "On which side to you dress" there and had not the slightest idea what he was talking about. Up to the war you could get a modest suit, two piece, for fifty shillings, and I did. Shoes were always bought from Archers at the entrance to Tithe Barn Street, the other entry to Caddy's and the toy shop Worfolks. Incidentally, that area behind Archers shoe shop, and between Caddy's and Worfolks was not always a scene of joy and pleasure which I depict. Late one night in 1931 on that site was found the body of Maggie Schofield, badly battered with a blunt instrument. Maggie Schofield did not have the highest of reputations, but it was a brutal murder which exercised the minds of the Dewsbury detectives, alas with no arrest and no conviction, a rare unsolved crime in fact. There was talk of bringing in Scotland Yard, as the practice was then sometimes, but there was no action. My father said he and other officers knew "who done it" but there was no proof. No forensic science laboratory had been invented then, or if it had it was in its infancy. By nature of my father's work footwear was important and he always wore Grenson boots, but always, and I was shod, as I am today in part, with K shoes. Always leather, maybe because synthetic plastics were not invented, or if they were they were restricted to Wellington boots, but even they were mostly rubber.

The toy shops were a child's dream. The main suppliers were Bickers, down a little from the Majestic cinema, and whilst the front windows facing Bradford Road and Cloth Hall Mill displayed furniture and the like, the side windows showed toys, Hornby trains in particular, especially towards Christmas. I got my first ever cricket bat from Bickers, but it was not very good and I suspected a hole in it when I batted. It was soon discarded. J and B's was opposite the top of the then open market, between the covered market and the Town Hall, in Foundry Street where it joins Corporation Street. They were good but Worfolks was the ultimate, a real Aladdin's Cave. It was next to Caddy's and my first Hornby train came from there. And Meccano, green and red it was. There was always a superb collection of toy soldiers, lead mostly then, model cars, aeroplanes, Meccano sets, kites, boats and everything little boys dream of. I certainly dreamt about them. I also got my first pop pop boat there, made of tin, about 3 inches long, mini boiler with in and out pipes from boiler to rear, and the whole set in motion by lighting a candle under the boiler and off she went, until the candle ran out, in the direction created by the tin rudder. Oh bliss, I kept mine for years. Its sea mileage was immense, not just in the bath, but on the lake in Crow Nest Park. It cost 2d and you can still get them today, if you know where to look, at £5.50 a time, made in Japan.

There were three main Arcades, two opposite the Co-op building, Kingsway and Queensway ending up at the top side of the present open market, and these had quality shops, no doubt about it. Heughans the chemists was there and with no national health service Mr Heughan managed to cure most minor ills at low cost. As a policeman my father got his medical care free, under the police doctor, G.H.L. Hammerton of Wakefield Road. He was known as "George Herbert Leonard" by everyone, something like the Russian use of the first name and patronym in talking to someone. That custom seems to have died out but was common then. My mother and I used Dr Jubb of Savile Town, who was reputed to have brought me into the world. At seven shillings and six pence, later twelve shillings and six pence a time, we didn't get there much unless we were very ill which was hardly ever, thank goodness. There was a lot of self help (which Virginia Bottomley or her successor might contemplate) and apart from Mr Heughan we were big on bread poultices, which consisted of slapping bread, soaked in boiling water, on the affected parts, even deep cuts and bad abrasions. The fact that your skin was burnt off around the injury seemed to count for nothing, and screams of agony were met by the following words, sung at a fast rate.

> Up comes the nurse with a red hot poultice,
> Slaps it on and takes no notice,
> Ah-ah said the patient, "that's too Hot",
> "No", said the nurse, "It's not not NOT".

Goose grease, rubbed into the chest for bronchial problems, was less painful, but smelly.

Woods the sports shop was nearby and whilst the display of cricket bats, balls and pads was supreme they were never in my price range, except for a pair of football boots once, the need probably arising at the time of the Co-op quarterly dividend. Wigfalls at the top of one of the Arcades sold bicycles and always had a good stock, Raleigh, Hercules and the like. I never got a new one there as my first two were second hand, but what vistas the arrival of the first bicycle, when I was 12, opened up. It cost £5, had drop handlebars, by Golly. Visits to

Ossett and beyond beckoned, provided the bicycle kept going without mechanical fault or burst tyres. The real specialists on bicycles were a couple of permanently oil stained (body and overalls) lads with premises along the bank of the Calder at the library end of Wellington road, and opposite the old central school (Victoria Centre) by the bridge to Savile Town. "Below" the Old Anchor pub describes it better. The shack in which repairs were carried out was always in imminent danger of falling down, and the two of them worked for a pittance for they were just enthusiasts. They could do anything with a bicycle, probably even make it talk. For pence only they could straighten or replace spokes, fix wheel rims, mend punctures, weld, or would it be solder, nipples on to brake cables, where the cable joined the handbrake, fix gears and chains. They had spare parts for every known cycle, British or foreign. It was almost a pleasure for something to go wrong with your bicycle, as you could sit and watch the Calder flow by as they mended and got you back on the road effortlessly. I do not think it ever occurred to them simply to fit a new part, the old had to be repaired and therein lay the magic. I once laboured half a day to get a cross threaded peddle off the shank and failed. I should have known better, and taken it to them in the first place, for when I did they had it off and repaired, a cross thread mind you, in minutes, at a cost of pence only.

The third Arcade ran upwards from Balance's flower shop (now gone) in the Market Place, opposite the Town Hall, to Corporation Street and Dempster Lister's bread and cake shop. It was unthinkable to buy flowers from anywhere but Balances for one simple reason. The Dewsbury Rugby League Football teams for Saturday 1st and 2nd XIII's, were chosen by the selection committee on Thursday night, and by 9am Friday mornings the teams' names were on full display outside Balance's. It was a meeting point throughout Friday as most of us argued that the team selected was another gaffe by the selectors, and our choice would have got a better result, frequently true, of course. Especially my selections. My parents hardly ever supported Littlewoods Football pools, but I was emboldened by my rugby know-how, explained later, to enter rugby league pools and had one decent win when I correctly forecast the results in eight games. I collected several pounds. I should have continued as I could have made an honest buck or two but did not, always finding a better use for the stake money.

That Arcade contained the Music shop, at the top, but it profited little from me as I only bought a couple of mouth organs there, for we were not really musical, although we had a piano and I had some lessons. If there was a shortage in our cultural education it would be music. It was in Leeds Town Hall that I first heard the Leeds Philharmonic Orchestra, or was it the Leeds Symphony Orchestra? They never visited Dewsbury as I can recall, but the Town Hall was used for dances which were attended as one got into late teens, and girls came on the agenda. Dancing to Les Driver, who lived in Hartley Grove, at the approach to the park, and his band was a highlight of the week on Saturdays. I had this propensity for treading on girl's toes which made me *persona non grata* with the prettiest and I was no fool; so I kept to the Waltz where treading on my partner's feet was reduced to a minimum though it still remained and does to this day.

At Hartley Grove we had a wireless or radio which was one upmanship at the time. It ran on an accumulator, whatever that was, and this had to be charged up once a week or so. I know there was acid in it and it had to be carried carefully. So, you got two accumulators, one being used and one being charged, all a bit messy. But came the day, about 1934, when my father bought an electric wireless set of which he was immensely proud. It never occurred to me before but the original with accumulators did not have wires, hence wireless. The electric one did, to the electric plug, so perhaps that was when "radio" superseded "wireless". Anyway, it came from a little shop up Bond Street and was the first Ultra set in Dewsbury. He paid cash and it was delivered, so all we did was plug in and switch on. It was a great piece of furniture, about 3 feet high and two feet across with just three knobs at the bottom, on and off, volume and station bands. Mahogany case too. Not that there were many stations, the BBC and one other, with the possibility of Radio Luxembourg on Sundays I think. This was important because that was commercial radio and Ovaltine advertisements loomed large. In fact I became an Ovaltiney, with a badge to prove it, at a cost of 2d by mail, and I could sing the Ovaltiney song, "We are the Ovaltineys, little girls and boys", with some gusto, especially in the bath. The routine listening for me was

Children's Hour at 5.15pm to 6pm (News then) with its various Uncles (Uncle Mac) and Aunties and family stories which always included a dog. My first dog, Raque, was so called after the Children's Hour dog. I graduated, over the years, to In Town Tonight and the Music Hall broadcasts which whetted my appetite for the real thing. I only ever saw my mother cry three or four times in her life, but I recall vividly her tears, streaming down her face, as we listened on our Ultra to the abdication speech by King Edward VIII. It had to be important for that display. But all was not lost, and the Dewsbury Education Committee always came up trumps, and schoolchildren got good free commemorative presents, usually commemorative books or beakers. There were beakers for the Jubilee Year 1935 (George V), Coronation 1936 (Edward VIII), and Coronation 1937 (George VI). I still have two George V Coronation beakers, now "collectables".

The photographer in town was Edgar Taylor in Church Street, or Mark Cross. It was mandatory to have photographs taken, in the days before the masses had cameras, or even when they had. The first statutory one was when you were a couple of months old, and you were stark naked on a rug on the floor. These could be used in later life to ridicule or humiliate you before the latest girlfriend if unapproved by the family, in an effort to dissuade her from having anything further to do with you. The second was when you made it to the church choir, and you had to be taken in full cassock and surplice with celluloid collar which tended to choke. Copies of these were sent to all relatives who, with luck, said "Ah" and sent you another postal order for two shillings and sixpence. The third compulsory one was also important, and was taken during the war when you were in the Army Navy or Air Force, and had made it to Lance Corporal or Second Lieutenant, it didn't matter which. The real reason here was that if you didn't come back, there was a picture for the *Reporter* to publish. If you could be seen, either as a Lance Corporal or a Second Lieutenant, with a couple of campaign medal ribbons, so much the better. It added colour. I was lucky again, as I always was, and had a Brownie Box camera, second hand, given to me as friends of my parents, the Lawtons, moved up market. It had a problem in that it took films 2¼ by 2¼ and they were displaced by films 2¼ by 3¼ over the years, but it took good photographs, and the Brownie was made to last as it did indeed, until about 1950.

I said my parents paid cash for the Ultra Radio, and they paid cash for everything. My mother always expected a discount for cash. It was old fashioned Dewsbury that said if you couldn't pay, you waited 'till you could. The only thing my parents bought on hire purchase was a garden shed, and I could feel the tension, and heard the debate, before the decision was made. A postal order for ten shillings had to be sent off every month and it was a blessed relief when the last payment was made, to my parents anyway. I must say the lesson was not learned by me and I was known to use credit, of necessity being my excuse. There was a time in my life when the children and I (I taught them) always saluted quite smartly every branch of the Midland Bank that we passed, on the basis that without that bank we would not survive.

Insurance was not seen as any advantage either, and none was ever taken out by my mother until the eighties. When my parents became house owners, instead of tenants, they still declined insurance and they saved hundreds of pounds, if not thousands, as they were never burgled and nothing dropped on their house from passing aircraft. They never lost anything, they damaged little, and the house never subsided—I suppose they were lucky. Alan Clark (of Diaries fame or notoriety, whichever way you look at it) has publicly indicated that all insurance is a racket and you don't need it, but then he is a bit richer than most of us. Banks also came in for the same treatment, ignored, except for the Co-op bank, and later the Halifax Building Society which held the family fortune; not the Dewsbury and West Riding Building Society in Church Street, surprisingly. That was a mistake too. My Auntie Clara, my mother's sister, who lived in Halifax, actually "went out" (as the saying was) with the then Manager of the Halifax Building Society, the Boss, for several years but nothing ever came of it and neither married. He told my mother about 1926 or 1927 that whatever she did, she was not to change whatever account it was she had with the Society, as it paid good rates of interest. It must have been 1984, when my mother was failing a bit, that I persuaded her to change that account, still paying the good rate of 2½% interest, to one that was paying somewhere in the region of 8%. At the same time I persuaded her to insure her bungalow against damage from aircraft and subsidence and the rest, largely on the ground that if I were to inherit, as opposed to the Cats and Dogs Home, I didn't want just a shell and a piece of ground. This was accepted most reluctantly and she still refused contents insurance. That relationship of her sister with the Manager of the Halifax Building Society was used by my mother to telling effect all her life. If there was any doubt about getting her hands on a Halifax Building Society calendar, much sought after and in limited supply, she pulled out details of the 'twenties romance, and nearly always got one.

There were several printing firms, but Ward's of Caxton Square were in the top league. It was run by Albert Exley and later his son Frank Exley, a terrific guy, ex Wheelwright school and a good and keen cricketer. He could work out most complicated arithmetic in his head, and you could say divide 3,560,636 by 4,375 and he got the answer without a mini computer, not then invented. Brilliant. He also had a business card with the words "Our competitors are a right shower . . ."

Chapter 3

We moved house again in 1935, from Hartley Grove
to Number 1, Malvern Road which was off Bywell Road.
The house was no bigger than the one we left and was
only two down and three up, two and a half up in truth,
and I got the half up. It had electricity and gas, a
bathroom and a lavatory, now called toilet. I heard it said
we had moved to a "better area" and the rent was twelve
shillings and sixpence a week, up a bit from before; I
know that as I saw the rent book. The rent was collected
by Miss Thompson, the daughter of the owner, who
confused my parents by bragging that she had been on
holiday for a week to some exotic spot, Cleethorpes I
believe, and had apart from the hotel bill, only spent
sixpence the whole week. She was a Scot.

For a 10 year old the real advantage was the garden,
some twenty five yards long, not garden *per se*, but
because the three feet high stone garden wall at the
bottom abutted the turnstiles, at right angles, to the home
of the Dewsbury Rugby League Football Club, Crown
Flatt. Above the wall was a gesture of a couple of strands
of barbed wire into which gaps could be and were cut. If
I hopped over the wall on the right, I was outside the
turnstiles and would have had to pay to get in. If I

hopped the wall on the left, I was in without paying. There were small gaps to the right and the left in the barbed wire strands and it goes without saying I used the one on the left, although later events made it no big deal. My parents indicated I could see the game from the back bedroom window, which was true, looking between the terrace to the left of the main stand and the terracing behind the goalposts at the Shaw Cross end. At the start I could only see three quarters of the pitch from the bedroom, and as the terrace behind the goal posts got bigger and bigger, a planned development to which the tipping of building rubble was encouraged, I could see less and less; I also complained that it was not possible to shout support from the bedroom as you could from the ground itself and that argument must have won the day because my father bought me a youngster's season ticket at five shillings. I had kept back the argument that being in there meant I could buy a mug (not cup) of hot Bovril or Oxo at half time for ½d from a small kiosk at the rear of the main stand. I could not understand why men rushed into the bar, opposite the Bovril kiosk, to get cold beer when they could buy hot Bovril. There was something weird about adults I thought. However, I was not complete. I had to have a Dewsbury scarf, and I started making the necessary noises. My mother, in common with all her friends, was a great knitter and wool came always from the Scotch Wool Shop in Northgate, a little below the Co-op building. Nowhere else, ever. Miss Vollans was a leading light there, and she eventually married P.C. Benn, and they produced Audrey Benn, who subsequently married

Gus Lillyman. Other policemen married girls from that shop, too. Talk about a closed shop! Anyway, the wool was bought and I ended up with a home-made magnificent job, fully six feet long, with tassels and with the colours, all of four or five inches deep, Red, Amber and Black. I still had it in 1950, and wore it, but by then it was getting a bit battered. It went four times round my neck.

Harry Fortescue was the secretary when I arrived, a nice and very competent man, but he left for pastures new about 1936 or 1937, when I was 13 or so, and Eddie Waring became the new secretary of the Dewsbury Rugby League Football Club, at 21 the youngest secretary in the Rugby League's history. It was an appointment with great consequences for the club and indeed for Eddie; the committee, which got team selection wrong most weeks, according to me and my friends, got this one right.

Eddie obviously had a Rugby League background and was involved with the Yorkshire Federation of Supporters' Clubs League, catering for youth sides. He coached the Dewsbury Black Knights team, a very talented lot of teenagers who mostly went on to league rugby a few years later. He got much glory over the years, and rightly so, but his brother Harry, who also lived in Malvern Road, was a rich character too. He was an electrician and brilliant. I saw my first television in his house, a screen fully nine inches square, about 1937 or so, black and white naturally. He had a most modest electrical shop at the bottom of Leeds Road, by Eastborough school, and could surely have run half a dozen shops if he had wanted to. Harry became a leading light in the Auxiliary Fire Service, which had taken over fire fighting duties from the Police Force some time before 1939. The parents of Eddie and Harry were friendly with my parents and lived a few hundred yards away in a bungalow in Chiltern Road which must have been near enough behind the Crown Flatt goal posts at the Shaw Cross end. Mr Waring senior became unable to walk easily, or at all, and as his walking problem coincided with the arrival of my first bicycle, with drop handle bars too, I used to change his two library books weekly at the newly opened Earlsheaton branch library. We were both big on detective stories at the time, Bulldog Drummond type of thing, and he said I never repeated a book, and I never brought one that he did not read through to the end, some feat from a small branch with not an enormous choice, though I know the branch topped up weekly from the main library to create change in their public offerings. There was always a bit I hated as I bid my farewell after the library run. Mr Waring would insist I took 2d for my trouble and in vain did I repeat it was no trouble but a pleasure and as I changed my own books at the same time, I was going anyway. I still ended up with that 2d as I tried desperately to get out of the door without it.

I cannot think how it started but I began to help out in the club office on match days. From age 10 I was always interested in what was going on there, and it wasn't just rugby. Russian Cossacks came to give displays of horsemanship that took your breath away. They charged, sabres flashing, at a series of turnips on poles and one after another the turnip heads came off, a dozen in a row. They rode stood up, sat down, upside down, three abreast, eight abreast, all in a line and even backwards. These were real Cossacks on tour from Russia, the end of the world to us. Of course the horses left their marks on the field of play (they were coralled in a corner of the pitch) and I later saw the groundsman, of which more later, nonchalantly raking it in on the basis the grass would grow better and I think it did. I know I would not have wanted to play on that field for a month or so, if then, but it was off season as I recall.

Just before the war North American baseball came to Dewsbury, an unlikely spot most would have thought, but a league was formed of about nine clubs in the West Riding. The Dewsbury team was led by half a dozen Canadians, real professionals, backed up by a few locals and Ken Turton's older brother, Arthur I think, played several games for sure. I quickly mastered the rudiments of the game and found it fascinating. Nine a side, a pitcher instead of a bowler, and the batsman had three strikes or four non-strikes over the plate to be out. The object was to hit the ball so hard that you could run round the five pointed diamond for a home run. Other players on intermediate points of the diamond could also run on every hit, in an endeavour to get to next base or "home" before the ball did. There were some glorious diving skids to base. I was too young to play but I practised with the team, got the feel of a baseball bat and whacking the ball, half as big again as a cricket ball, a fair old distance. If you were fielding you had a big right hand glove only, and to catch that ball I know you needed it. Unfortunately that all petered out as it was not financially viable; people attended and paid to get in, really for novelty value, but it was not enough.

But back to the rugby. On match days there was a routine for getting the gatemen, part time regulars, to the turnstiles at the two entries to the ground and the two stands two hours before kick-off, but I got the job of going to the turnstiles and the stands with the Customs man—I never knew why him, but it had something to do with tax—as the game was ending. We checked the number of clicks on the individual turnstiles, noted by the Customs man and me, and we later used my check against the takings of the gateman, in cash. At first it was 6d to go in, 3d for children, the aged and unemployed. With a gate of 5,000 and 10,000, not uncommon then, especially for cup ties, there was a lot of silver and copper to be counted as the gatemen brought it in to the office under the main stand. So three of us would count the lot and bag it, five shillings for copper and two pounds or five pounds for silver in stiff paper bags. There were some ten shilling notes but one pound notes were rare. We checked each gateman's takings against his turnstile clicks and whilst there were minor discrepancies, nothing serious was ever discovered. One gateman was not invited to officiate again but that was as much as it was over several years. These paper copper and silver bags were then placed in linen money bags with a note of their contents for Eddie when he did the banking. Mostly there were several

hundred pounds in these canvas bags and you would
have thought it went straight to the bank, but it didn't.
Eddie had a two up and two down cottage in Old Bank
Road—I think it went with the job—and the cash was
deposited under the stairs in Eddie's house until Monday
morning when the banks opened. It wouldn't do today,
that's for sure, as some bounder would be forced to thieve
it. Nobody ever did then.

The rewards for all this were enormous. Firstly the
other counter checker and I (and Eddie if he was free to
help which he wasn't) got a free tea, brought in on a tray
from the tea room by the bar by the nice tea lady, and
three shillings and six pence cash. I was rich beyond the
dreams of avarice and I knew even as a boy of 14 or so,
that Dewsbury families, not many but some, were living
on a wage not much over two pounds ten shillings a
week.

Occasionally I had to double as car park attendant,
take the cash and direct parking. We always had a
policeman there for some reason but he never did much.
I did not care much for these car parking duties, even
though I still got my three shillings and six pence. The
trouble with pre-war motorists was that they tended to
be a bit snooty, and some even parked (absolute
bounders) on what was later to become my cricket pitch,
at the bottom when they were directed to the top end. I
got out of car parking as soon as I could. I also graduated
to travelling with the team to away fixtures in the team
coach. I was a kind of Minister without Portfolio, and
lent a hand at whatever was needed, maybe helping to
push the kit basket from coach to dressing room. It let

me see a lot of the Yorkshire rugby league grounds, and
I saw my first barrage balloon over Hull on a visit there.

After WW2, when fate (my father and George
Ferguson) decreed I was to become a solicitor (I take no
responsibility for it myself) I had—horror, horror—to
read for law examinations and I spent countless evenings
sat in the main stand. I took my dog Basher over the
garden wall (left) into the ground and the stand where I
read Snell's "Equity", Chitty on "The Law of Contract",
and other equally ghastly law books, without which no
examinations would ever be passed. There was indeed a
time when I thought even when I did read them, the law
examiners would not be defeated, but they were in the
long run. Basher, of course, had a wonderful time, with
the whole ground at his disposal, but he never strayed
far. He was a main stand dog. He would bark at me after
an hour or so, as if to indicate I had studied enough for
one evening, and we ought to get back to a ball game.

I was saddened on a recent visit to see the stand gone,
and the ground given over to a housing development.
Bully for those who will live there and I thought the
houses were nice and not squashed up too much
together, and the owners will surely be buying a bit of
history. It must have made economic sense for Dewsbury
to share a rugby ground with Batley, but all I can say is
that it would not have done in my day. Batley were the
foe. I hope the new stadium at Owl Lane is successful
but I bet there will be no Oxo or Bovril at half-time, at
½d a mug.

I used to train occasionally with the team, and the second team which was very strong, on Tuesdays and Thursdays, and what a team they were in the late thirties. Alf Chester at full back who could kick goals from any angle and did. Years later I saw him at the County Hall, Wakefield, where he was a senior attendant looking after the needs of Sir Bernard Kenyon and other senior county council officials. Jim McTiffin, a prop forward of immense size and strength; a giant of a man and hard as nails, but I once overheard him in a conversation about rough play which I should not have heard as a boy. "I am not going out there to injure anyone, certainly not for thirty shillings a game", thirty shillings being the maximum lawful payment per game under early wartime rugby regulations. He was rough but never a dirty player, and he later turned to wrestling. Billy Wood came up from one of the two London clubs which had been formed, Acton and Willesden or Streatham and Mitcham; he played wing and was so fast as to be unbelievable, but admitted to my father he was a bit frail for rugby league. Bill worked for the Yorkshire Heavy Woollen District Transport Company, first as an inspector and later as a senior executive. Arthur Veysey was another flyer, playing on the other wing, a dark swarthy man, extremely fast from a standing start. Gil Morgan played loose forward and was capped by Wales. Gil later coached Earlsheaton amateur rugby league club, where I played a few games.

When I left Dewsbury I moved first to Buxton, in Derbyshire, and played rugby union there and always thereafter, which I thoroughly enjoyed. By chance I had

mentioned to the captain that I had once played rugby
league as an amateur, but that I never received a penny
for playing wherever that was, which was true. I had
obviously impressed some county selectors in club
games, because I was invited to take part in the next
Derbyshire county trial. In telling me this the captain
was quite adamant I must not indicate in the slightest
way at county that I had played "league", even in the
forces or as an amateur, as they were very strict locally
and it would unseat me. I never did mention it but I saw
a type of apartheid in the flesh. The rules have been
altered a bit since then and a former amateur rugby
league player is not barred from rugby union. It is
otherwise for former professional players, and even in
June 1994, Dave Hinchliffe, a Labour Member of
Parliament, introduced a Bill in the House of Commons
to authorise former professional league players to
participate in Union games. He will not succeed just yet,
the establishment is too strong, but maybe by the
centenary of Rugby League in 1995. We all know of the
rumours about what happens about payment in rugby
union in South Africa, Australia, New Zealand, France
and Italy, to name but a few.

Harry Royal played scrum half and must have been
just about the best scrum half in the league at that time.
Eddie was very active in the transfer market and got
many players trials with Dewsbury, some of which didn't
work out. Brendon McNamara came and went and Roy
Francis, one of the first coloured men I knew, a gifted
athlete if ever there was one, played centre for a season
or more. If accommodation was a problem it was always

found for new players, and the last two lodged with brother Harry in Malvern Road for weeks at a time. There were several players who had been miners, hardy tough players who always gave 100% on the field.

In 1939, the New Zealand Rugby League side were touring England and Wales, led by George Nepia, the famous Kiwi fullback. When he kicked for goal after a try under the posts, he never stood up after placing the ball, he just kicked it from the crouch position. I had never seen that done before and tried it myself one day, achieving absolute failure as the ball, going straight alright, never got above six feet high. He was actually an amateur until he came to live in England in 1935 and played first for Streatham and Mitcham, and then Halifax. He also played baseball for Streatham Giants.

The New Zealanders played just one game as war was declared, before returning home. That was against Dewsbury the day before war. Eddie had a movie camera, no doubt borrowed from his brother Harry, and I had never seen one before, but nevertheless was asked by Eddie to take the film of the players, Dewsbury and New Zealand, coming out of the tunnel on to the field of play. I was honoured to do it and felt quite important, but I never saw the film on screen, the war and all that. Dewsbury lost. A year or two later Ineson Blakey, himself no mean performer on the rugby field with Wakefield Trinity, and then a detective in the Dewsbury police gave me the New Zealand tour badge which was in silver, with a kiwi on a leaf, "NZRLF 1939" inscribed, the whole on a long lapel badge pin. It was a prized possession but eventually I sent it to Eddie for the Rugby League museum where it should still be. Michael Blakey, Ineson's son, became a first class sports reporter himself, and worked for several Yorkshire newspapers, and later the nationals.

The war brought a relaxation of all the rugby league rules about player registration, and it gave Eddie a chance to exercise his entrepreneurial skills and bring to Crown Flatt a whole galaxy of international stars, including the famous Jim Sullivan of Wigan, then coming to the end of his great career but still a force to be reckoned with, even if he was not so fast around the field. He must have been 40 then, but could tackle hard, was difficult to stop on the run, and could kick goals when necessary. Alan Edwards and Jim Kenny from Salford appeared regularly, with other top class players who then rapidly disappeared from the rugby scene into the armed forces.

The nearest I ever got to Glory and Dewsbury 1st XIII was about this time. Travel was difficult, and with players travelling from Lancashire and beyond, late arrival by players was common. For one game I was actually stripped and changed to play (on the wing which was thought less dangerous for a (just) 17 year old) when the dashed player turned up by taxi 5 minutes before kick-off. Quite spoiled my day he did.

The rugby club physio and "sponge man" was Herbert Smithson, who was of the old school. Unless your arm or leg was actually off, or hanging off, he used Wintergreen, which was bought by the club in very large tubs, half a hundredweight at a time I shouldn't wonder, but then I suspect they bought nothing else except a minimal amount of bandage and sticking plaster. Why something called Wintergreen was always red puzzled me at first, but you only needed a couple of applications of it to cease to care. It nearly burnt your skin off, and soon your skin colour matched the red ointment. Wintergreen kept internationals going for the last twenty minutes of any game, and kept me going for 30 minutes or more. I doubt Herbert Smithson had any medical qualification, other than first aid, but he was first class at his job and whilst I've seen him pull out dislocated fingers, he knew when hospital was needed, via the ambulance which was always there, with St John's ambulance men, on match days. He seemed to be the kit man too, responsible for laying out clean shirts with the right numbers on, and boots of which there was always a good supply for training and indeed for playing, unless you had your own which the internationals certainly had. I used club boots.

The other character in the *dramatis personae* when I arrived on the scene was the groundsman called, what else, Milner Oates. He must have been knocking 70 when I first knew him, and he had a mane of white hair, down over his collar, and it was never cut methinks. I think he did trim his drooping white walrus moustache. He was fully five feet tall, if that, and he wore the same clothes all the time I knew him, several years. He must have had something different for Sundays, but I never saw him on Sundays to check. Communications were not as good as they should have been in those days and he was not told that I was *persona grata* at the club and had permission from the secretary, no less, to play cricket and football in the lower car park with my friends. Mr Oates took his job seriously and one day shouted to me from inside the ground, by the running track, "Git aht o' yon cloise" which interpreted actually meant, would we be kind enough to vacate the field. My cousin, Geoff Stapleton, who was staying with us and playing with me, had led a more sheltered life in Wakefield (Wakefield was thought by Dewsburians to be a bit "refeened", whereas Leeds was wicked: Huddersfield was "not talked about", except for Fartown, tractors and Huddersfield Town soccer) and could make neither head nor tail of the request until I translated for him, whereupon he shook his head at our weird and wonderful ways. But all was well as I explained the position to Mr Oates, and we played happily ever after. The other communication problem was how to tell the punters who had won the prizes, a bottle of whisky usually for 1st prize, and maybe chocolates for others, for purchasing the match programme with the lucky number on it. This was solved by chalking the numbers on a board which was then paraded at half-time around the perimeter of the pitch on the shoulders of two men, fore and aft, for all to see. It was Mr. Oates' job, with one other, to organise this after the numbers had been chalked on. One match day there was a shortage of the "other", and I was conned into it. Mr Oates was forrard and I was aft and we set off. But because he was five feet tall, if that, and I was six feet plus, the board was at an angle of nearly 45 degrees, and you could see the paying customers twisting their necks to see the numbers. This neck twisting was accompanied by caustic comment, even before we reached the far side open stand, to such an extent that I resolved on the home straight to the main stand, never again to assist Mr Oates in his task, and he would have to find some other "other", if you understand. I never did convey the happy tidings to lucky programme winners again.

I don't know what measures are taken today to keep the rugby pitches fit for play in icy or frosty weather, underground heating perhaps at some of the top grounds like Headingley. But in the thirties life was more basic. The Dewsbury club bought bales of straw, dozens of them, from friendly farmers and these were stacked, about November, round the ground but inside the railings. Any sign of frost three or four days before a game, and certainly before cup ties, with their enhanced gates and gate money, had Milner Oates unbaling and spreading the straw, several inches thick, across the entire pitch. It was extremely effective; it was cheap because you could use the straw more than once unless the wind caused havoc with it unbaled, and blew it around, and it saved countless games and the gate money. There was never any shortage of helpers to remove the straw, which they did with giant wooden rakes some two or three hours before kick-off. If the straw clearers got a bit behind in the work, men from the crowd, who had actually paid to get in, would lend a hand in the last half hour. I would like to think they would do that today, but I doubt it.

About this time, or a little before, I was fortunate enough to meet the famous Lyman brothers, Joe and Jim. They were members of the record breaking Dewsbury team of the twenties which won many trophies, all the trophies in fact. Jim kept a pub, the Woodman, at the bottom of Hartley Street, opposite t'abattoir, and frequented by my father when we lived at Hartley Grove. Jim's wife was a charming lady and I think she was a school teacher before marriage. She lent me her copy of Tom Sawyer which I had not read until then, Mark Twain being somewhat of an unknown quantity to me. To my shame I never returned it and I still have it. I can only hope that if young Joe, their son, reads this he will communicate so I can return his mother's book, even though some 60 years late. Jim Lyman later kept the pub at the bottom of Daisy Hill, next but one or two to the (now) Yorkshire Building Society in Church Street, the Market House. It was at Jim Lyman's Hartley Street pub that my father took to drinking "half and half", half of bitter and half of mild, mixed, and mostly Tetley's which was a good drink and still is. He compounded the problem by smoking pipe tobacco comprising half an ounce of Bruno and half an ounce of Flake, which led me to accuse him, when I was old enough and dared to, of being indecisive and not being able to make his mind up. He soon got his own back, by accusing me of the same thing when I joined the Royal Marines. I couldn't make my mind up, he said, and was I a soldier or a sailor? He was joking I think.

It was many years after all this, about 1981, that I met Eddie when I was in Leeds, giving a few lectures to younger lawyers about recent law changes. By chance I dropped into the posh bar at the Queen's Hotel which was Eddie's haunt for many years, and we met for the first time in twenty years or more. We reminisced for an hour or more about the old days, his jobs at Dewsbury and Leeds, his father's library books, and my three shillings and six pence a week for modest clerical duties. Eventually the conversation took a serious turn and he asked me outright if I, as a solicitor, would take on his tax affairs as he was in just a little difficulty over tax, largely due to rugby jaunts to Australia and somehow America. I expressed sympathy, as one would, but indicated that I held a public office job and was a bit restricted in what I could do, but in any event, I could not accept the brief because I was writing a book, I had lecture commitments which went beyond reason, the criminal justice system in which I was involved was going to the dogs (it always was and always is) and my presence was needed occasionally at my own office. More, I said I was working harder than I ever had, just to stand still. It was like water off a duck's back, and he persisted in asking and I persisted in declining until he played what he thought was his trump card. "Take on my tax affairs", he said, "and I will pay you double what I paid you last time". Whereupon we collapsed in roars of laughter and the barman must have thought we were mad.

When Eddie left Dewsbury he went first as secretary to the Leeds Rugby League club at Headingley, and he had started writing for the *Sunday Pictorial* as rugby correspondent, but he really arrived I reckon when the BBC decided to televise rugby league and was clever enough to appoint him as commentator. "Oop and Under" is now folklore together with going for "an early bath".

"It's a Knockout" seemed to follow naturally as night follows day, but I shall remember him best (quite apart from the three shillings and six pence weekly) in the Morecambe and Wise show. That was the Eddie we knew, enjoying life, and giving enjoyment to others.

I lost track of it all in the fifties as I had to concentrate on my own career, but I worked it out Eddie must have been at Leeds Rugby League club when Jack Myerscough was chairman there. Jack served for many years at the Leeds club and was very popular. He married Margaret Dobson, who was the daughter of Nurse Dobson who lived next to my family at Malvern Road. Nurse Dobson was the old fashioned District Nurse type, full of medical knowledge, with unbounding kindness to those in her care. I knew Margaret as a real cracker of a girl, full of fun and vitality and extremely attractive to boot. Alas, she was about 10 years older than me, so romance was out (damn) and there were boy friends galore. But Margaret and I were friends, notwithstanding our age difference and she took me to many places, including my first trip to Belle Vue, Manchester, to see motor cycle racing on the cinder track, where the exhaust fumes made you cough and splutter but it didn't matter it was such fun and exciting. We also went to Golden Acre Park in Leeds, and did the boating, the swings, the dodgems, the lot. All this was made easy because all her boy friends had cars, and she would only go with them if I went too. I must have been a gooseberry and resented by the boy friends, but they never showed it. Her tragic death must have been a terrible blow to her family and friends, as it was to me when I heard months later and was even then hundreds of miles away and long out of touch.

As the war got under way, if not a bit before, the training and fitness at Crown Flatt came under the wing of Harry V Smith, the North of England middleweight wrestling champion, the most charming of men. Barely five feet tall, but with the muscles of a six footer, I have seen him bend a three foot iron bar, fully two inches in diameter, above his head. He was a popular strong arm performer at garden fetes and carnivals. He was a fitness fanatic and he took on a lot of Home guard unarmed combat training. He died prematurely just after WW2 and it was a sad loss to Dewsbury. He also took charge of "Keep Fit" held at Crown Flatt on one night a week, for an hour or so. This was a war time effort to make the country health conscious, and the public were invited to join in free of charge. Attendance was patchy, no doubt because there were many other commitments we all had, but I got there when free. Because of a couple of low attendances, only a dozen or so, I was emboldened to write what was my first letter to the press. I wrote to the *Dewsbury Reporter*, around which our world turned, and complained quite bitterly about the poor attendance at the "Keep Fit" classes and indicated that the war could be lost unless Dewsbury bucked up and got there for a few physical exercises. I wrote anonymously, and whilst not signing "Disgusted of Dewsbury", it was something like that. To my pleasant surprise the Editor published the letter and that was a big day. Over the years I have had a couple of letters published in the *Times* and *Telegraph* under my name, but nothing equalled that first one in the *Reporter*. I could even have turned to journalism after that, but I chickened out after some further journalistic efforts turned to ashes.

Charlie Pickles, who also lived in Malvern Road (we must have been a knowledgeable lot) was the sports editor of the *Reporter* and wrote all the rugby reports. I doubt he ever had a holiday, and certainly not in the rugby season. He had a special place, centre stand, at Crown Flatt, and a thoughtful committee (or Eddie Waring) saw that he had a piece of wood, nailed in front of him at 45 degrees, upon which to rest his notebook. That was the full facility made available. Charlie's reports, a week late of course, because the Reporter came out on Saturdays, were eagerly read and extremely good copy. I think his views on team selection coincided with mine and those of my friends, but he was too much a gentleman to say so in print. I simply cannot remember him "knocking" any player, and to write praising a good game by any player seemed to be natural to him. If a player had a bad game it was dealt with gently or not mentioned at all. Nor can I remember him ever knocking the referee, even when the rest of us were casting doubts about the eyesight, or even parentage, of that unfortunate official. Charlie's reporting was in accordance with the fashions of the times and all the better for that.

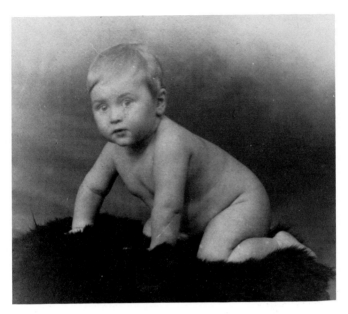

The author at an early age.

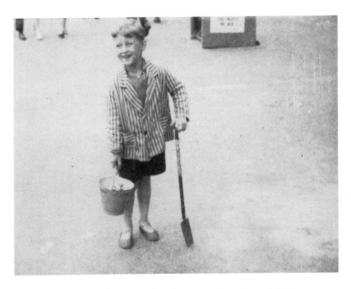

The author at St. Annes-On-Sea 1931.

Carlton Road Junior School
(Mixed) – the class of '32.

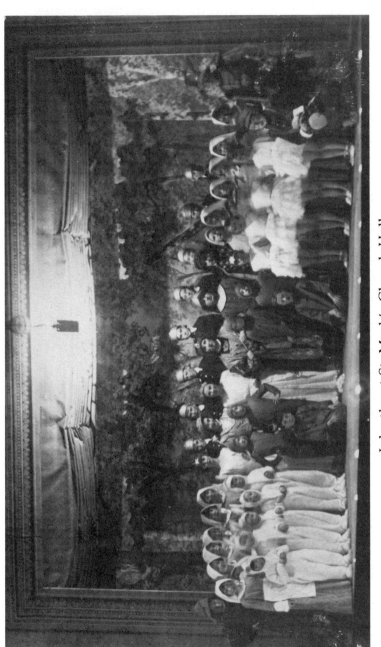

Iolanthe at St. Mark's Church Hall, circa 1934.

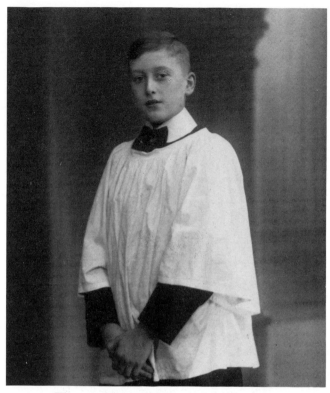

The author in 1935 about to collect
postal orders for 2 shillings and 6 pence.

Dewsbury Black Knights Rugby Team 1935.
Coach Eddie Waring.

Wheelwright Grammar School
Cadet Corps 1940.

Tupper Winder
about to commence
flying training,
1942.

George Nepia,
New Zealand
Rugby League star,
1940.

Wheelwright Grammar School Old Boys Cricket Team, about to depart on Whitsun Tour, circa 1947.

Dewsbury Coat of Arms

Chapter 4

The family move from Hartley Grove to Malvern Road in 1935 necessitated a change of school, to Earlsheaton Junior (Mixed) a delightful little building, still standing and used as St Peter's Church Centre, at the corner of Earlsheaton, near the road which dips down to Chickenley, and with superb views across Pildacre. It was also within one hundred yards of an old building on the opposite side of Town Street, in which cheap (very cheap) boiled sweets were made. We bought them, broken rejects anyway, at ½d for almost quarter of a pound at the vehicle bay entry. From Earlsheaton Park, the bottom corner and also nearby, the views over Dewsbury, towards Mirfield are simply panoramic, and it is one of my favourite spots. Alas, the academic achievements of Earlsheaton Junior (Mixed) were not high in the eleven plus stakes and I distinguished myself early by failing the equivalent of the eleven plus examination as did most of the class, if not all of it. There was talk at home of me going "dahn t' pit" which I thought a bit extreme. Luckily, for me, the Dewsbury Education Committee ran what was called an "over age" examination, a further chance for us later developers, some 6 or 12 months on. Whether or not thoughts of t' pit affected me I know not, and doubt it, but this time the examiners were held at bay and an offer of an education at the Wheelwright Grammar School for Boys was made to me, under the hand of the Education Officer, Mr Emerson, no less. His son P.K., was later to become a class mate and colleague. Still, the chance of this education must have been a close run thing, as Sir Jeremy Moore said of his victory in the Falklands. I seemed to develop the knack, in later life, of just doing enough to scrape through examinations, and there was certainly one occasion when I was quite convinced the examiners had mixed up my examination papers with some unfortunate called either Moir or Morris or somesuch, who failed because he got my marks, and I succeeded because I got his. That was one of the law examinations.

So, the Wheelwright Grammar School for Boys in Halifax Road (Motto *Res Non Verba*—Deeds not Words—and which I honestly tried to live up to, not having to try that much in the Royal Marines) became my seat of learning for the next few years. There was though one further hurdle to overcome. The Wheelwright, even though "taken over" by the council Education committee in 1922, was in fact then a fee paying school, with a two form entry of some fifty boys annually at 11 plus. Of the fifty I think about fifteen or so were fee payers, and that would leave thirty-five scholarship boys, of which I was one, where the Education committee, the ratepayers anyway, picked up the tab and paid the school. The Education committee ran a scheme whereby their scholarship boys had the parents cough up something towards the fees, according to means but with an overall top limit. Most of my contemporaries came from homes of very modest means, though not all by any means. My parents were assessed at twelve shillings and six pence a term, that is thirty seven shillings and six pence a year and I overheard my parents discussing this problem of payment and its effect on the family budget. I knew my father earned £5.12s.6d. a week, with a monthly allowance on top of that for rent and boots and whatever, and if you ask how I knew that, it was because I had (and have to this day) an enquiring mind and needed to know what was going on, so I rifled all their drawers for financial documents when they were out, to get such information. Funnily enough my daughter has inherited this need to know facility, I used to allege from her mother, but I cannot sustain that accusation now.

It was decided that the fees could be afforded, but unfortunately it allowed my mother, over the years and when in one of her Mrs Bucket (Bouquet) moods, to tell all and sundry that she and my father had paid for my education. I have seen my father shudder at such disclosure but there was little he could do, or he would have been banned from something or other, possibly the garden, or access to the bank statement. There was a clothing list which did not seem to cause problems and I assumed it coincided with the quarterly Co-op dividend; I was very proud of the football shirt and shorts (they came just below the knees in those days) and was not averse to the school blazer with badge. Travel was discussed and the rules were not dissimilar to todays, over three miles and the Education committee paid for it, under three miles and you did your own thing. They measured that three miles as the crow flies, so even if you needed two buses, as I did, down Leeds Road (1) and up Halifax Road (2), it did not qualify for free transport. Luckily the Yorkshire Heavy Woollen District Transport Company had foreseen all this and provided a "Contract", not to kill anybody in the accepted normal meaning of that word, but whereby, for fifteen shillings a term, you could travel *ad lib* on their buses. I had one of those for the first year or two and became very mobile with my feet, my bicycle and my "Contract".

There was one other mode of transport I was lucky enough to try. My mother's sister Ivy married an entrepreneur, Bob Huish, in Halifax who either owned or had access to his employer's pony and trap. This was a magnificent affair, and I travelled more than once from Dewsbury to Halifax by pony and trap. It was a three seater trap and a bit bumpy, especially over cobbles, but most exhilarating. It must have been a bit damp if it rained but I can only remember fine weather drives.

At first sight the Wheelwright Grammar School for Boys looked quite forbidding, when seen from Halifax Road, matched only by the forbidding appearance of the Headmaster, "Keff" Sadler, a big six footer who ran a tight ship. But neither the school nor the Head were what they seemed when you got in there, and I still have the fondest memories of all that school did for me, not least on the playing fields. Keith Waterhouse relates his truancy in Leeds when he was young, and his guilty conscience made him think the school attendance officer (the school bobby) was always after him, so he dodged in and out of Leeds market to avoid detection. It never even occurred to me to truant and I shot off each morning to absorb what was on offer. In any event I knew the school bobby so he held no terrors for me; he was the father of my Hartley Grove friend, Fred Blackburn, who somehow ended up at Heckmondwike Grammar School, which was puzzling as he was a Dewsbury lad. Howard Blackburn was immersed in the Parish Church, the amateur football league and its administration and was quite small and wiry. There was a great day, just post war, when he, together with Cyril Eaves the probation officer, ventured into darkest Ravensthorpe to find out why the son and heir of the lady of the house had not been to school for a week or two. Note a week or two, not months or years as today. Madam, known as a bit of a card, hence the two of them, had seen them coming up the garden path, and as she opened the door she let fly with the proverbial custard pie. Howard ducked easily but Cyril, rotund and of bigger girth and not so quick on his feet, got it full in the face. Talk of summonses for assault was rife, but nothing came of it, as the officials were far too sensible, and I was told the son and heir did resume school when his chicken pox cleared.

But to the Wheelwright. It suited me fine, a six day week, but Tuesday, Thursday and Saturday afternoons for games, or free, but often Saturday morning games when you made the 1st or 2nd XI football and cricket teams.

I was elected form captain the first year, and indeed after that in each year, followed by house captaincy the last two years. I had not had such honour before and I had no idea what it entailed but I soon found out. Poor "Tat" Tattersall, a class mate, died aged only 12, and I had to represent the form at the funeral, my first, at Earlsheaton Church and cemetery, followed by the funeral tea at Bailey's cafe. I was a bit choked and upset, but his mother was so kind to me as I stuttered and stammered my condolences, and I could not have been much help to anybody. But Duty had been Done.

It also led to being Editor of the form magazine which was a complete disaster and took six months to produce less than 50 copies. The copy was good enough, produced by the form intellectuals with jokes, an article on stamp collection, football results of the form team (published just after the end of the following cricket season) and even poems by either Stockdale or Buckley.

I knew what to do, as I read it up, and enquired of other budding form magazine Editors. I got some of that jelly stuff and the special ink, so in theory, if you wrote your copy in the special ink on special paper, you could imprint that on the jelly which had been melted down and poured into a flat tin bigger than the paper. You then rolled blank paper on the jelly, pulled it off and there was revealed your work, in as many copies as you liked till the jelly ran out.

Without her knowing it, I got hold of my mother's Yorkshire pudding dish, well, one of them, put the jelly in and put it in the oven where it caught fire and burned. The second lot leaked from the tin and covered the oven bottom, and the third lot refused point blank to produce any copy at all, perhaps because it was a bit thin on the dish bottom. There was not much jelly left and then the ink ran out. I was not popular with my mother. I was a right idiot, because at that stage I should have shown leadership, and then delegated the whole lot to someone like Brendon Grimshaw, but I did not know of his journalistic capabilities at that stage of the game. In fact I started to type the magazine on my father's typewriter, one finger stuff, and as I could not afford carbon paper (the whole capital had gone on jelly, ink and paper) it took months. Looking back it must have been about that time I decided on a career as a lion tamer, of which nothing came; being an Editor went out of the window and so did journalism.

After the retreat of the British army from Dunkirk in 1940, there were occasional war weapons weeks, when everyone was supposed to dig deep into pockets for money with which to buy weapons to win the war. I came up with a scheme for the form which was quite popular and unusual. A Mills hand grenade then cost four shillings to make, and the army was short of them, so I floated the idea that we might buy a few. This idea took off and every Monday morning, every class member had to produce 2½d to me and the whole, about four shillings, went off to the government to buy grenades. It indicates the class size was about twenty. In itself it was nothing, but no one else had thought of grenades, and it is symptomatic of the time that that spirit was everywhere. No one ever failed to pay as I recall it, and the scheme lasted for well over a year, before it gave way to something more ambitious.

We were thrown into the deep end, academically, and whilst we were not used to that high level of concentration and sheer hard work, most of us survived, one or two children only dropping out inside the first year. I thrived on it, even though I am a bit thick by nature and certainly intellectually lazy. There must be something in those famous words about a healthy mind in a healthy body.

Walt Seed was the French master, and he must have despaired of us sometimes when our Yorkshire accents crossed the romantic French. Barrington Browne took Latin and whilst he had seen it all before, he certainly got the message across and I still aver that you can learn as much English grammar from Latin as from studying English. Mr Browne was the Second Master, in effect the deputy Headmaster, and was reckoned to have owned the finest collection of old silver in Dewsbury. English literature was taught by "Father" (not pronounced like farther) Franklin who was noted for his communist views, alas religiously kept away from us when some of us wanted to know about it. He never so much as breathed the word communism and more's the pity. Not in his brief must be the answer. "Father" Franklin was also a known atheist, but he still took classes for religious knowledge on some occasions. I expect he did his best. H.M. ("Jimmy") Docton knocked English literature and English grammar into us very successfully. After a year or two with him we actually knew about split infinitives, alliteration, hyperbole, onomatopoeia, metaphors and similes. Ask today's children of the meaning of these things and you get blank stares. It could be I am asking the wrong children but I fear not and they simply do not know what you are talking about. "Jimmy" Docton was also Commanding Officer of the school cadet corps which was great fun and made us aware of modest discipline, a first for some. Caradoc (Doc) Williams introduced us lower forms to mathematics in its forms of arithmetic, algebra, geometry, trigonometry and the like, but you had to watch his right hand which was deformed after he was shot at Paschendale in WW1, and like a piece of iron. He could give a fearful blow behind the ear with that hand, worse if you were not expecting it. He was from the Valleys I think, and today might well be called one of the statutory Welshmen. Dr Down was intellectually brilliant and made history live, for me anyway. He introduced us to the museum, and thereby some local archaeology, in Crow Nest Park. He also took charge of the chess teams at appropriate times. "Conk" Chester and C.M. ("Dai") Jones took physics and chemistry respectively, but I was not into those two subjects much, only enough to scrape through whatever examinations were current. "Tommy" Boyer also took physics at senior level. He had one speciality if you were inattentive or worse; with his index finger and thumb he got hold of your hair over your ear and twisted.

Harold Perkins took senior maths, along with the Headmaster "Keff" Sadler, who concentrated on the sixth form. I don't think the Headmaster liked me much, early on, but perked up interest, for he was a cricket addict, when I made the 1st XI cricket team at an impossibly early age. I took a wicket, hitting the outside of the off stump with a beauty that just swung back to do it, with the first ball I ever bowled for the 1st XI at Leeds Modern. Oh Glory. "Keff" was umpiring a 1st XI trial at school one day, a bit before my glory at Leeds Modern, and was at the bowler's end as I faced one of the school's better fast bowlers, coming down the hill. I faced a pretty torrid over but scampered a one off a snick off the last ball of the over. "Keff" turned away to square leg, but paused and said "You didn't know much about five of those, did you?" He had a habit of screwing his eyes up and I thought he couldn't see very well. He could, and I could only answer his question in the negative. I could have said I didn't know much about the sixth, either, but didn't. It quite spoiled my day. Mind you, Barrington Browne could be caustic. One year I ran a couple of good heats in the 100 yards on Sports Day. It was a House based games and B.B. was my housemaster. He came up and said "Well done", as I was not expected to do so well, "A tip", he went on, "When you are out in front like that do not look behind you for the opposition, keep running." Came the final which left me well adrift, and he again came over, and indicated he needn't have bothered with the previous advice, there was nobody behind me, they were all in front.

After WW2 it was Harold Perkins who took the Old Boys' Cricket team on the popular Whitsun tour. He played cricket for Thornhill in the league and was a very crafty left arm spin bowler. The tour was usually Amersham, Chesham, Hounslow and Marlow, Harold's home area. These were marvellous days, good fun and some good cricket. In one game our captain came over and whispered I was not to appeal for LBW or any catch behind the wicket as the opposing captain came in to bat. This was a bit strange, and not the way I played nor had I ever had such a request before. In the bar after the game, I was discussing the problems of post war travel with a member of the opposing team, petrol rationing and all that, and great difficulty getting to away games sometimes by 'bus even. He told me all,. There was no problem for them, as the captain, who had made a bob or two in his aircraft production factories during the war, realising the difficulty for his club, had bought two taxi firms locally, and the taxi firm petrol was used for their away games. We later had drinks in the captain's house, on the banks of the Thames with the motor boat moored at the end of the garden and looking at the sheer luxury, it would not have surprised me if he'd bought three or more taxi firms. I'm glad I did not appeal: no need to spoil a good thing. It was on another tour when, being an opening bowler and a bit quick, I bowled out an early batsman, knocking his middle stump backwards some six or seven yards. Maybe more. Harold wandered across, I thought to congratulate me, and dry as ever as slow spin bowlers sometimes are, he commented "Yes, but it's only straight up and down stuff you bowl".

"Pluto" Bradshaw and Mr Cooke took art and music respectively, but these were dropped after year one for some reason. Mr Cooke was a disastrous disciplinarian, the only one, and it was difficult to assess his musical capabilities, suspect, I would have said. The machines on which for 2d you could punch a message on a metal strip were in vogue in the thirties, and we created one "Made by the Greeks" and actually nailed it to his piano. He didn't even see it, or pretended not to, and it completely demoralised us.

Miss Gilbert was the only lady teacher and I think she was a relative of "Keff" Sadler. We had a touch of geography from her and that then disappeared from the curriculum, not just for me but for everybody. Pity that, as she was a good geographer, but she did keep disappearing from the classroom during lessons, which did not do her stationery supply any good at all, as we raided her cupboards for unused notebooks relentlessly. There was in fact a small fee paying junior school in the building, a prep school in effect, where Miss Gilbert assisted, but the teaching there was undertaken mainly by Lt. Commander Robinson and Miss Newton.

I could understand woodwork being dropped after a year as that was not thought academic at the time. A Mr James took that and I managed a kettle stand and a magazine rack in the year. The kettle stand has gone the way of all flesh but I still have the magazine rack, a bit of good oak that. However, I am not allowed to display my handiwork to visitors to my home, and it is hidden away in my little study, but still used daily. Mr James was writing a book on woodwork for children at the time and I appeared in the book in a photograph, clutching a dangerous looking chisel. My enemies said the photograph was merely an illustration of how NOT to do something, but I hotly denied it. Pride was at stake there.

Captain Pickles was a favourite of all of us, even those who were not keen on physical activity. He it was who christened Harold Fowler as "Ikey". He took all physical training in what was a comparatively new gymnasium, annexed to the main building and opened in 1936. Three times a week for forty minutes was the minimum P.T. requirement, and no excuses allowed unless your leg was actually coming off. A loosening up first 10 minutes of arm and leg swinging exercise, followed by wall bar work, or on the horizontal bars was the norm. A bit of jumping over the wooden horses, followed by climbing up the ropes, and so it went on with never a dull moment. The showers were compulsory after this and the school laundry bill must have been enormous. Captain Pickles held only a part time appointment as P.T. master and I am pretty sure he was or had been a career officer in one of the Yorkshire Regiments after service in WW1. His other job intrigued most of us as he was the secretary of the Castleford Rugby League Club, and we got him to tell us about Castleford, where he lived, and the Castleford team players, who we then compared with the Dewsbury team. The result of the Dewsbury versus Castleford game was always discussed at length with a bit of gloating if Dewsbury won. We were much quieter when Dewsbury lost.

It never ceases to amaze me, that 50 and more years on, I can still remember some of the basics we were taught. "Towns, small islands, domus and rus take the ablative". Thus rus–Rure–in the country (Browne). "Surely you know the difference between a metaphor and a simile—remember one example of each" (Docton) "Change the bottom sign and add" (Williams). "Julius Caesar never said that, boy, it was Cassius" (Docton) "You will learn this poem by heart by 10am tomorrow, all 12 lines of it, or else" (Franklin). Probably

> I must go down to the seas again,
> To the lonely sea and the sky,
> And all I ask is a tall ship
> And a star to steer her by.
>
> And the wheel's kick and the wind's song
> and the white sails shaking,
> And a grey mist on the sea's face
> and a grey dawn breaking
>
> And the rest

Richard of York gained battles in Vain—red, orange, yellow, green, blue, indigo and violet (Chester on the spectrum).

That magnificent teaching staff needed administrative back up, naturally, and part of it came in the presence of Doreen Hullah, the school secretary and daughter of a local bookie. She was a big girl. Miss Hullah never simply walked into a classroom, to consult a master, she made a dramatic stage entrance, slow, dignified and carrying all before her. As pupils we were all agog for one of her state visits and any thoughts of the antics of Julius Caesar, or quadratic equations for that matter, went straight out of the window, until she moved off like a ship of state to the next port of call. The school surely owed a great deal of gratitude to Doreen Hullah for the smooth way the school functioned; she was always calm and never panicked, as she picked her way through the hundred and one school problems with an expertise second to none and gained over many years in the job. She knew all our names too. Virtually all her work was carried out behind the scenes and you would never have known if there was a crisis anyway so smoothly did it all run. I suspect today she would have two or three typing staff to help her, a receptionist, a bursar to handle finances and no doubt a social worker or two and at least one education adviser; she did the lot on her own. I learned later she married a Polish fighter pilot and all I can think is "Lucky Poland".

Physical punishment was on the cards in my day. I never suffered it, but came perilously close in the early days. It was usually six of the best, across the bottom, inflicted by "Keff" Sadler with a cane, kept conspicuously on view in his outer office. I was never once smacked or otherwise punished physically by my father, or my mother either. Charmed life or something, I must have had. The words "He's nobbut a bairn" were in common usage to excuse much juvenile behaviour especially in poorer families.

Next severest punishment was "a Thursday" which meant reporting for work for two hours on Thursday afternoon, when the rest were at games or otherwise free. I had a few of those, and I found it just irritating when there was so much else to be done. Writing essays or copying from some great work was the task on "Thursdays". Further down the scale were ordinary

"Detentions" and this meant staying after school for about one hour to read or write about Shakespeare or some other improving literature. There was an alternative in the cricket season, when ten or so little boys had to roll the cricket pitch, by hauling the heavy roller up and down for the hour. I opted for that when I could but it wasn't our choice; it helped selection by being "a big lad". I swear that wicket was truer after a good rolling by the detainees, than ever a mechanised roller could do it; it was certainly flat.

The school manual staff was thin on the ground, but very effective. The caretaker was Jack Wilson, a former army senior NCO with a local regiment, and who seemed to have spent most of his life in India. He was tattooed on the arms which occasionally evoked comment, as it was unusual. He had a very talented family, very pretty daughters, and at least one of the boys became a graduate. He was also the groundsman and kept the four football pitches, two in front of the school, and two on the top field, in excellent condition. The goal nets and white line markings were usually immaculate, certainly on the bottom two pitches. The cricket pitch, between the lower football pitches was likewise kept in good shape, and fenced off in the football season to avoid undisciplined feet causing damage. The only advantage he had was an endless supply of detainees for rolling the wicket.

Roland "Tupper" Winder was the assistant caretaker when he should have been a pupil. When the war got a year or more old the fifth and sixth forms had to produce five fire watchers each night, and they, together with one caretaker and one master, had to put out incendiary bombs with stirrup pumps if the school was hit and caught fire. I luckily drew Sundays and did duty with a super group of friends, different masters, but always Tupper. We used the caretaker's cubby hole in the basement as our headquarters, because there was a gas cooker nearby and fry ups were allowed as a change from the packed sandwiches. But the evenings were notable for Monopoly which we played every Sunday until 2, 3 or even 4am on Monday mornings. No enemy incendiary bombs were ever dropped on school; we should have been extremely annoyed if they had, especially Tupper, as our Monopoly would have been interrupted. Just occasionally a bottle of wine was procured by us, nothing to do with Tupper whose conduct was always quite proper, and imbibed during the evening. It was a grave error that some wine got spilled down Jimmy Docton's desk one night, as he was a teetotaller. We actually saw him sniffing his desk next day and we knew there was to be a real stink about it when the Headmaster was also seen sniffing the desk. The Saturday night schoolboy firewatchers were thought, on balance, to be a bit more tearaway than us Sunday nighters and suspicion fell on them. As sheer chance had it nobody asked us outright who had done it, as we would have been bound to admit it—I think. It died down and we were well out of that we always thought. It had an effect in that we all stuck to tea and coffee after that.

Poor Tupper, he volunteered for flying duties in the Royal Air Force, and became a Sergeant wireless operator/air gunner in bombers. His aircraft was shot down over Germany about 1944, and his body was never found. My ship had been damaged about that time and I got a few days leave whilst it was repaired, quite unexpectedly. Tupper had lived with his mother, a lone parent, in a house off a yard, about half way down Leeds Road on the left. I called to see her and found she'd taken it as well as she could, but she was devastated and his death was a great loss to her and the many, many friends he had. I last saw him in the Fleece in Northgate (now long gone), when previous leaves of a few days had coincided once, a few months earlier. He was singing away, quite plastered, round the piano with friends, after his first few bombing operations were completed successfully.

Our academic life continued apace, both before and after the war started. Having survived the first year, thoughts turned to passing the school certificate examination, the equivalent of 'O' levels today, but it seemed a long way off. Extra mural activity was there for the taking and it was education in the real sense had we but realised it. There was the debating society, meeting fortnightly, and I once seconded a motion that this House "believes all jazz music originated from the tom-toms of Africa". I thought my leader and I argued it all rather well, but we lost, miserably. The chess club was popular and met at least weekly, sometimes in the lunch hour as well. Considering I was a bit thick by nature, I took to the game surprisingly well and became the school junior chess champion, beating Brendon

Grimshaw in the final which was hotly contested. The prize for the winner was a book on chess which I still have; the prize for the runner up was a pocket chess set in a leather wallet. The sheer irony was that I wanted that pocket chess set and not the book, but fate decreed otherwise. We were too competitive, even then, not to try for the top position. I made the school chess team at about 15, and we had several eight-man team fixtures with other schools nearby. Dr Down was in charge of the team and our keenest rivals were Heckmondwike Grammar school. I think I got a draw in my first game for the school, against Heckmondwike, but it was a good day when they were beaten as they sometimes were.

The Cadet Corps took up much of our time, increasingly so after the war started. Before that it was much more fun, I suppose. There was an annual cadet camp at Filey for a week under canvas, as the saying went. Ten bodies to a Bell tent, feet to the middle. We were attached to the King's Own Yorkshire Light Infantry, so we knew all about marching at 140 paces to the minute, instead of the normal army pace of 120. We had a regular army Company Sergeant Major attached to us, and a later one was Company Sergeant Major Brown, who lived in a short street, off Halifax Road, I think Albion Street. He too had spent much time in India with the British Raj and had an attractive daughter called Irene. It was Irene who taught me that telephone boxes were not just for making telephone calls which I stupidly thought they were. We were out carol singing one eve shortly before Christmas and we got into this telephone box together at the top of Bywell Road. I forget why. As she said afterwards, there wasn't that much room and it was natural for me to put my arms around her. That in turn put our faces quite close together, and she said it was quite natural for me to kiss her, and as she enjoyed it, as I did, we kissed more than once before returning to the more mundane task of carol singing. I reckon she was the first girl I kissed but it was like ships passing in the night, as we lost touch with each other (literally) and I never saw her again.

In addition to the CSM we had an old army cook with us in the Filey camp for the week. He too was ex KOYLI and that regiment had its own way of cooking bacon, amongst other things. I there learned that it was best done over an open air army fire and fried as slowly as it possibly can be. This fried bacon, with eggs and fried bread, was a masterpiece and we lived on it for a week as we found out the old army cook could not manage anything else. He was good on bread, butter and marmalade or jam as well, but then he had shot his bolt. One year the tents next to us were occupied by workers on holiday from Rowntrees in York, and they brought with them a very large quantity of chocolate, which they let us buy at knock down prices. I formed a love affair there with whipped cream walnut whirls which we bought at ½d a time when the retail price was 2d, so by and large, with the bacon and eggs and whipped cream walnut whirls we got by. I think we did a bit of arms drill, PE and map reading but the regime was relaxing I found.

Back at school the cadet corps met on Fridays, pm, when we paraded up and down a bit, and were inspected

by the C.O., Jimmy Docton. At first we had WW1 puttees
over breeches a bit like riding breeches. You wound this
khaki cloth roll, about 4 inches wide, round your lower
leg, overlapping it from ankle to the bottom of the
breeches and then tucked the end in somehow. I never
got the hang of that and my puttees always ended up
round my ankles leaving a bare bit of leg showing. That
was the first intimation I had that clothes and my shape
body do not coincide; I mean any clothes, puttees,
morning suits, evening suits, ordinary suits or leisure
wear, and I have had to learn to live with it. My family
indicate I am scruffy but I resent that, it is just that tailors
do not make clothes to fit my shape. It was a good day
when we got ordinary army trousers.

We went on exercise often, mostly at Briestfield and
Shipley Glen. Why Shipley Glen I know not, but I have
attacked that Glen in Infantry formation more times than
some have had the proverbial hot dinner. I have also
defended it, often successfully. I know that if the
Germans had ever attacked Shipley Glen, and I had been
on the other side they would have had a sticky time of
it, shot to hell are the words that come to mind. Quite
unlawfully I bought my first half pint of bitter at the
pub in Briestfield, when aged just 15. We were on exercise
there when Sergeant Major Bilton and I became detached
from our attacking (or defending) main body. It was
raining heavily and we thought we might just as well
eat our iron rations in the pub as in the rain, and
sauntered in nonchalantly asking for two half pints of
bitter, Tetley's, knowing that normally we would have
been thrown out at 15, BUT we had uniforms on and

possibly looked like the real thing. Anyway, we got the two halves which set us back 5½d each. I never looked back after that and thought it was the making of me.

Certificate A was the academic aim in the cadet corps, guaranteeing an army commission it was said. The Royal Marines had not heard of it. At least twenty of us got it in my year, with extremely high marks (said the Army Officers conducting it) in drill, drill instruction, use of firearms and map-reading. Well, some of the map-reading test was on Briestfield and Shipley Glen and we knew every blade of grass there. We used the drill hall (TA) at the bottom of Halifax Road for rifle firing, in the .22 range there in the basement. Half a dozen of us became very proficient indeed and reached marksman and sniper levels of marksmanship, no mean feat, to be used later in the real army or other services.

The cadet corps was exceedingly democratic for its day, and under Jimmy Docton's leadership. There was a time when I was quite put out about lack of promotion and complained somewhat bitterly about it to the C.O. Next day I was promoted to Sergeant.

Sport was dominant though, and all four soccer pitches were used every Tuesday, Thursday and Saturday. Masters refereed all games and time for sport was not the problem it appears today, the masters simply accepted it was all part of school life. I fail to see what the fuss is about today over whether games are to be compulsory or not. The great majority of my school friends were mad keen to play and there was strong competition for school representative sides, and even,

come to think of it, the form sides. There were many
who were not sport orientated and there were ways and
means of opting out if you were so anti sport. I think no
child is, and whilst he may not wish to play rugby,
football or cricket, let him have a look at tennis (available
to us in courts round the back of the school) or athletics
or swimming and something will tempt him, when he
finds he is good at something. Boxing was not on the
agenda in my time but one or two showed some interest
in karate which seemed to be making a first appearance.
After form football, the next aim was the Colts (under
14) side, then the House side, through the 2nd XI to the
1st XI. I worked through that progression and had more
than a couple of extremely happy years of 1st XI soccer.
Once you became a regular member of the school 1st XI,
at either football or cricket, "Colours" were awarded and
they were keenly sought. I got both and very proudly
displayed the badge on my school blazer. It had a white
background whereas the school badge was red and black.
We were different. The 1st XI sometimes played at home
on Saturday mornings if not afternoons. Apart from
pupils we had a regular band of followers, a few old
gentlemen from the area and a few potential girlfriends
from our sister school, the Wheelwright Grammar School
for Girls, only opened in 1933, just up the hill. Betty
Boothroyd, the Member of Parliament for West Bromwich
and Speaker of the House of Commons was a supporter
and Betty Lockwood, who was the deputy chairman of
the Equal Opportunities Commission later in life, also
came to view occasionally. I forget now who was sweet
on who but I think Betty Boothroyd liked one of the

Beaumont boys. We all had one or two forays together as we realised that girls might matter, one day, and we should have to talk to them. It never seemed to get much further than talking, apart from the telephone box.

The school had a very good fixture list which is not surprising as we were not bad. We had coaching from the York City coach every two weeks or so. We had opponents like Leeds Modern School, Rastrick Grammar School, Royds Hall, Huddersfield Technical College and the Quaker School at Ackworth. Apart from the quality of the football, most schools were judged on the quality of the teas after the games. Ackworth always came very high on the list, probably because it was a boarding school, and was big on sausage and chips with bread and butter and tea, or milk. Maybe because Ackworth ate so well they were very robust in play, unless you got there first, which I quickly learned to do. But not until I had had my legs scythed from under me several times. It was true that having hacked you down, the Ackworth player always apologised profusely, and gave you a hand up, especially when he saw your blood flowing. I thought Quakers did not like violence until then. I had obviously been misinformed.

We were very well served at our own school by Mrs Ellis, who provided teas more than adequate after games against other schools. School dinners had not arrived pre-war and we all went home for dinner (not lunch) on most days although there were only 3 days with an academic working afternoon; provision was later made for space to eat sandwiches and they fitted neatly in a gas mask box if you took the gas mask out. Alas, to do that, and be found out, was, I think, a capital offence. Or nearly that.

Foul or obscene language was never ever (but once) used on the field of play, or off it for that matter, and I find today's bad language openly used by professional and amateur players, in football especially, but even in rugby union, quite unacceptable and totally unnecessary. I am no prude, and have been known to swear on occasion, but when every fourth word is an obscenity I find it too much, and I would ban such players even though I know I have a minority view. That such language goes on in front of girls and ladies watching just aggravates it all, to me. The only swearing I ever remember at school was Ding Franklin, just once, when I shouldered him off the ball, probably violently and unlawfully, at a time when shouldering, well defined, was allowed. That was the only one in some four or five years, playing some field game two and three times a week. I can remember no dissent whatsoever over any referee decision, maybe because referees were masters, but we all thought any errors evened themselves out.

The coach for away games, again courtesy of the Yorkshire Heavy Woollen District Transport Company, and often with two teams aboard, never exactly hurried to foreign parts which suited us. I spent many a happy hour on the back row (away from younger players who were not to be corrupted) playing "odd man out" with half pennies. It needed three to play, the coins were tossed, and the odd head or tails took the other two. You could play for almost one hour on a journey, and still end up winning or losing two pence. That it led to a profligate life of gambling and worse could be true of some.

I played school football at various times with some class players. Vic Metcalfe, who went on to play for Huddersfield Town for many years, later a coach or scout there, was one. He had magic feet, could beat two or three opponents by sheer speed, and had the ball in the net before anyone knew it. He was an all round sportsman and I played cricket against him once at the Hanging Heaton ground, where he hit me for five successive fours or sixes, some into the next field. Woe was me. One of the Mitchell boys was a better player still, I thought, but went on to window cleaning and property dealing and no football that I heard of. "Ding" Franklin, the son of the teacher, was a giant of a man, handsome and always bronzed which we thought was the result of an infra red heater type thing. He was centre half, ever at the place where the ball was, and dominated most games in midfield. He read medicine and became a psychiatrist, which sub consciously I must have held against him. The Morris brothers were sport personified, good at all ball games and variously captains of school teams. Gil Ramsden was a talented ball player, neat, tidy and forever dribbling and twisting his way past three or four opponents, before unselfishly passing the ball elsewhere for the scoring of goals. He became a successful business man in Leeds and was a magistrate in Dewsbury. Marcus Fox thought he might have had some socialist tendencies at one time—oh dear. Stuart Richardson, brother of my form mate "Tich" Richardson, and son of the Borough Treasurer, was a goalkeeper of considerable merit. Always athletic, he became a parachutist during the war and spent some hair-raising months when he was dropped over France behind enemy lines to join up with and help the maquis disrupt German supply lines. He survived, eventually to become the colonel of his local T.A. unit in South Yorkshire, where he was a senior solicitor with the Coal Board. He was articled to the Town Clerk of Dewsbury in 1946 when I was later articled to the Magistrates' Clerk, and part of his job was to come and ask me for the committal papers when an accused was sent for trial at the then Quarter Sessions in Wakefield, now the Crown court, as the Town Clerk prosecuted for the local police. One accused called Shuttleworth was so committed for burglary, but the case was a bit out of the ordinary in that it was alleged (truly I guess) that in addition to the burglary of Burtons, The Tailor of Taste, he had tried to have sexual intercourse with a female dummy which had been displayed in the window. Without thinking, when Stuart made his duty call on me, I said "Ah, here are the papers for Shuttlecock" and it took a few seconds for it to sink in, whereupon we both had a good laugh. Unfortunately it stuck, and most of Stuart's papers to the barristers involved, and the Quarter Sessions court, were headed "R. -v- Shuttlecock" instead of Shuttleworth, but we survived. Just.

A lot of the footballers also played good level cricket, which seemed only natural because they were just good ball players. A different group seemed to emerge in athletics, the year of which terminated with school sports day, eagerly awaited even if you were not good enough to get to the finals, hotly contested. Most of the senior school were entered in far too many events, ranging from the 100 yards, 220 yards, and on to 880 yards and the mile, with discus throwing and throwing the cricket ball in for good measure. We never had javelin throwing which was probably wise and saved some nasty accidents. On a day of its own was the cross country, run annually. My father thought it might strain the heart for very young runners but was over-ruled. The entire school ran, and I doubt if a dozen of 300 boys were excused. Leaving school, the field turned left into Halifax Road and then left again up Healds Road and on to Mirfield church, where the return journey came via Dewsbury Moor and ended at school coming down Birkdale Road. It was something over six miles and a lot of us did it under the hour., some much over it. I cannot remember anyone giving up though many were reduced to walking at some uphill stage. I was. Peter Green was the king here and won it, easily, more than once. I saw him finish once, white as a sheet, but he had broken the school record which had stood for 30 years or more. I cannot be sure of the time but I believe it was somewhere in the region of 38 minutes. The first thirty got points for the House, thirty for first, down to one for the thirtieth. I felt I had done well to get in the first thirty even, and noted the small wiry ones often triumphed.

Apart from sport, there were a lot of what today would be called academic high flyers, with an emphasis on mathematics and some science subjects. I used to have a theory that all the high flyers "blew up", and ended up in dead end jobs, but I was wrong. The good middle of the road stuff achieved heights undreamed of, but the high flyers often succeeded extremely well in life. None that I know of actually ended up in prison.

I lost track of so many, as they did of me, but I know that Donald Williamson became a dermatologist of national repute. Gus Lillyman was on extremely important work at an atomic science plant in Scotland. Marcus Fox is the Member of Parliament for Shipley and surrounds, and is also chairman of the 1922 back benchers committee at Westminster. Staunch conservative though my mother was, I doubt she would have ever voted for Marcus. I would tell her, even when she was in her eighties, that I had had a pint (or a gin) or a meal in London with Marcus, and her reply never varied. "He'll come to no good; when he was on his way to school with his twin sister, he used to wallop her with his school satchel." Marcus and his sister must have been 12 or so at the time but he was never forgiven for what my mother saw. The Reid brothers were clever in the scientific field and held important posts as I understood it. "Ikey" Fowler a one time cadet corps sergeant major, and later one of the youngest captains in the Indian Army, had a successful solicitor's practice in Huddersfield. "R.B." Crowther probably had the plum. When he came down from Cambridge, he took a teaching job at the Wheelwright School and remained there for many years. Lucky RB. What he thought of the school's change of status in 1974 I never dared ask outright.

Of my own immediate contemporaries, Jack Brooke and I were friends for years, and he was last heard of chicken farming in North Yorkshire. It was "Brookey", a big lad, who came up with the idea of getting into Crown Flatt rugby games without paying, by going early and as he approached the gates, he held up his right arm to the gateman, bent at the elbow and showing three fingers, and said "Player", guessing the gateman did not know who was playing that day. I never found out whether he actually tried it or not. Donald Hemingway and "Butch" Firth were part of the Ravensthorpe contingent, good footballers both. Donald eventually moved house to live near me, and was my cricket and football partner in the rugby ground car park, with Gordon Penman from the Art college. Donald emigrated to Australia about 1947, which I am sure he enjoyed. Australia must have benefited. Gordon Penman was a bit more affluent than me in 1946, and he bought a new cricket bat, always a big day. He sold me his discarded Wally Hammond one, about five years old, for five shillings and I used it until at least 1966, making a few runs here and there, with more than my share of sixes. The splice then came away from the blade and I considered suing the makers for shoddy workmanship, but finally took no action.

Brendon Grimshaw was an enigma. He was always in the top three for English grammar and literature, but 24th or 25th (of 26) in all (but all) other subjects in which he had no interest whatsoever. He became a journalist with the District News, graduated to London newspapers and eventually became one of the Editors of the Kenya

Times. Whilst in Kenya he bought outright the island of
Moyenne in the Seychelles, and was allowed to keep it
on terms even after a socialist/communist coup in the
late seventies when the Prime Minister of the Seychelles
was in England. The island of Moyenne is about 1 mile
off Mahe, the main island, and some three quarters of a
mile from the island which is used as a prison. The regime
there is relaxed and one of the prisoners swims across to
Brendon's island from time to time, and there finds a
can of fizzy lemonade hanging on a string in the cool
water to drink before the swim back. There is nowhere
to escape to, so the guards don't mind the swimming
prisoner. I visited Brendon some 5 or 6 years ago, on the
pretext of finding out who really was the best chess
player, some forty or more years on, though we never
played in fact. I was quite surprised when he told me he
had actively disliked his last year or two at school and
had truanted and run away so often his father had to
take him away. This was news to me as I thought I knew
it all, but I didn't know that. His mother died in
Dewsbury, and his father then joined Brendon on
Moyenne, only to die there but after several happy years.
He is buried on the island and it was a moving moment
when we put a branch of bougainvillea on the grave,
not least because Mr Grimshaw had been friendly with
my father for many years. Creole cooking is the speciality
there and is first class with a strong Indian (curry) bias,
but big on fish. The Seychelles has a funny mixture of
people, white, light brown and black, being sat alone in
the middle of the Indian Ocean. Indians came south to

the islands, Africans went East to get there and at various times the French and the English had colonial interests.

A friend of mine who was a Lieutenant in the Royal Navy, when serving on a frigate, actually took the first white bull there about 1955, after the merchant navy said it could not be done from Mombasa. It was apparently an hilarious few days as jolly jack took it all in his stride, and there was competition to act as the bull "steward" the bull being crated normally but allowed out on deck for walkies. On arrival at Mahe the vet certified the bull was in good condition with no sexual hang ups (the point of the export) and that breed of cattle on the island today all stems from that white bull. Giant tortoises abound on the islands, living often for a hundred years or more. There were two outside Brendon's bungalow on Moyenne, called Bo and Derek. About the time of my arrival a baby giant tortoise appeared quite unexpectedly out of the bush, which proved that Bo and Derek had been up to what the white bull was sent for.

I was greatly honoured when asked if it could be called Cliff and I readily agreed; it was later christened with Seybrew, the Seychelles own produced beer. Words of caution were uttered by my wife who wondered whether I could be made responsible for its keep as it was named after me, but it appears the law of the Seychelles does not require that.

The Seychelles has its own Rotary club of which Brendon was a member and I attended the weekly lunch, held in my hotel as a matter of fact. I won a bottle of wine in the raffle, had a superb lunch, and then we got the speaker, whose subject was tuna fish about which I knew nothing. He was an expert, no doubt about that, and went on to explain, with evidence, that you could fish those waters for ever, even dredge 'em out for a hundred years, and the supply would not dry up. So, the crunch point was the need for another canning factory. The speaker was approaching this climax when it happened.

I should explain that the hotel restaurant was actually on the beach, and separated from it only by a wooden wall, some three feet high, but no glass windows which were not necessary in that climate. The speaker had his back to the beach and we sat facing him showing much interest in the further canning factory, when behind him, on the beach and crossing the window space left to right (it was a wide window), appeared five or six dusky maidens, topless, bouncing along (in all senses of the word) with a beach ball. It could be that the speaker had gone on too long, as happens at rotary meetings sometimes, but I doubt it. All I know is that there was an immediate lack of interest in tuna fish, and indeed canning factories, and the meeting broke up in what I can only call minor disorder. It was the best Rotary meeting I have ever been to, and I have been to a few over the years. It was a bit surprising too, as the government of the Seychelles had let it be known it did not approve of topless playing and bathing, certainly by European lady tourists. Maybe the rules did not apply to the locals or they were otherwise defying authority. I thought Good for them.

The Tolleys seemed to provide a succession of boys for the Wheelwright, as did other families. I worked it out it was better to be an only child, which prevented masters tut-tutting at poor or modest performance on the basis the older brother(s) would have done much better. We formed a secret society in our early years, of which "Tid" Tolley was a leading member, and we met in a disused shed in the overgrown garden of a house in Sugar Lane, reached by climbing through the rear hedge. We were there quite illegally by trespass but that added to the adventure. It was run on the lines of the Black Hand Gang and it was there that poor Gledhill, a red headed lad, was given the nickname "Freaky Boswell", and there must have been some literary connection which I never understood. How I loved that house with the overgrown garden; it was about 200 yards from the Dewsbury side entrance to Crown Flatt rugby ground, now modern semi-detacheds. Most of my life I wanted to buy it but fate took me away. Once in adult life, about 1946, it was for sale and I went and viewed. It was stone built, and had between a half and an acre of land and views across Dewsbury out towards Mirfield. There were stone slab floors downstairs and I think then only cold water. The roof was suspect but who cared, and it was only 200 yards from the rear Crown Flatt entrance turnstiles. I would definitely have stopped 12 year old boys meeting in my shed and blocked the hedge entrance, and otherwise have been quite beastly to them—I think—or would I?

Derrick "Jacko" Jackson lived in a terrace house, a couple of hundred yards from the Earlsheaton end of Bywell Road, towards Dewsbury. His mother and sister had a stall on Dewsbury market but it could not have been clothing, as Jacko was by nature practical and did not go in much for clothes. I would hesitate to say "scruffy" but like me, I think his clothes never fitted somehow. I last saw Jacko in ill fitting naval uniform, a chief petty officer, doing technical work of con-siderable importance. He was certainly better off than "Fatty" Sykes.

A German boy called Kneusels joined us in year one, his father working in Dewsbury on "high tech" equipment. He was a nice lad, but no footballer or cricketer. That family returned to Germany in 1938 or 1939, amid some allegations the father might have been a Nazi spy. I often wondered whether some of us might have bombed him, or shot at him a year or two later, or indeed whether he shot at us. I hope not.

Harry Parkinson (the youngest sergeant-major in the British army) and Jack McAvoy, a class bowler on the cricket field, were the mainstay of the Earlsheaton contingent.

Chapter 5

I suppose we must have got into mischief at some time or other, but I cannot recall much of it. If we did, it was never malicious, nor harmed anybody, except perhaps Jimmy Docton's alcohol sensitivities. A lad I knew suggested we ran a chicken business, breeding and selling, as he knew where we could get a few chickens to start with. This was worth exploring, but it was only when we got to some allotments at the top of Willans Road that I realised he meant me to steal a few, whilst he remained under cover. I dropped out of that sharpish. My father was friendly with the Broadheads (pronounced Bro-ad-eeeads), who farmed at Thornhill, and I spent many days on their farm with their son Harry. His elder brothers seemed to do all the work but I was there at harvesting time, which was also rabbit killing time as they all congregated in the middle of the corn field, and the square got smaller and smaller. Rabbit pie for days there was. Milking time was of interest and their change over from hand milking to machine milking I recall. You could learn words like beast and silage and mistal, but better still I was allowed to ride what must have been a shire horse from the fields to the farm. Harry and I once devised a lawful system of making profit from chickens by hatching out the eggs ourselves over a lighted candle which we bought from a nearby shop. Alas, the eggs never hatched out in the hour or hour and a half we allowed (it was then supper time and we never missed that at the Broadheads—or indeed anywhere else come to that) and it all ended in failure, unless boiled egg counted as success. I only hope Brookey fared better with chickens than I did if he really did chicken farm in North Yorkshire.

I do not think I was as mischievous as my father, who, on his own admission, in his youth used to buy a few lemons with his friends, cut them in two, and then stand sucking them in front of the wind instrument players of the Ossett Town Band, when performing outside Ossett Town Hall. This had the dramatic effect of making the trumpet blowers create excess saliva, then to "slavver" (that's the word they used) down the mouthpiece whereupon the music ended with drums only and in chaos. I wanted to try that out but the only brass band music we got was in Crow Nest Park on a Sunday evening, but where the bandstand, quite magnificent as band stands go, kept the public at bay and some 20 yards away. It could be that band stands were built as a result of the Ossett experiences.

This story is about Dewsbury, but Ossett does come into it as my father was born there, and his mother lived there virtually all her life. I visited her when I could over the years, as I liked the tram ride, the bus ride not so much fun. The family were Wet Wesleyans, with their own pew in the chapel near the Town Hall; my father claimed the "wet" bit merely so he could have a pint on

Sundays and other days when he felt like it. I doubt my grandmother ever touched a drop as a result of her mother hitting the bottle hard in what must have been about 1890 or even before. I know this because I have a copy of the will, dated 1914, of my grandmother's father, keeping the loot, of which a surprising amount was in property in Wakefield, row after row of houses, away from his wife and the evils of drink to the benefit of his children, including my grandmother, and in turn my father. But Ossett. In WW1 Ossett raised a company, if not a battalion, of infantry, Kings Own Yorkshire Light Infantry, as towns and areas were asked to do. Kitchener needed them. They duly paraded in front of Ossett Town Hall, a bit ragged but ready for embarkation to France to be shot at. The Colonel gave the order "Fall out the Officers", whereupon at least half the company or battalion simply slouched off the parade to rejoin proud mothers, fathers, brothers, sisters and other hangers-on who were viewing the proceedings with interest. The Regimental Sergeant Major was furious and tried to rectify the ghastly scene by getting the soldiers back on parade, but all he got was a complete refusal, on the ground that the Colonel had actually said "Fall out the Ossetters".

With a widowed grandmother in Ossett, and because I enjoyed the tram ride and then the bus ride at ½d a time, I found afternoon tea with grandma very pleasant. She lived at Westfields, with superb views across to Horbury, and ate well. Her teas were usually ham or tongue, with thin sliced white or brown bread and butter, and two or three different jams, jelly and cakes home made. Quite a prize. At 10 or 11 I stayed one or two weekends, and all was well until my cousin Geoffrey Stapleton also appeared for the weekend and we enjoyed ourselves, even attending the chapel Saturday Annual Fayre, where there were short Laurel and Hardy films, bran tub lucky dips, more tea, cucumber sandwiches, cream cakes and so on, all paid for with 1d or 3d tickets bought by grandma weekly over the previous year. Unfortunately, on the following Sunday morning, before breakfast, Geoffrey and I had a pillow fight in the bedroom. He gave me a real humdinger whereupon the pillow burst, and feathers, real feathers, cascaded all over the bedroom. We'd blown it. It was made very clear that we were both very welcome to stay in the future, anytime, but only so long as we were not there together. We never did go à deux again.

I had a bit of a set back academically in the third year at school when I was demoted from the 'A' stream. There was no argument allowed, we wouldn't dare, but it meant I had to drop Latin at which I was more than competent, and which I enjoyed. When I was later conned into training to be a solicitor it cost me dear, something over a year in time, because a minimum requirement even to start law training then was a pass in the school certificate examination in Latin, an 'O' level today, and I had to study it to that level specially before even starting off as a pupil. Luckily I had the grounding for it.

My father also had a set back as he was banned from the garden about this time. He could do heavy work like digging and path laying but nothing else. It came about because my mother had bought some rather expensive plants at the Allotment Association, the cost was five shillings or more, and my father was directed to plant them when mother went off elsewhere. When she came back she found eight plants had been duly inserted in the ground and beautifully tied with string, twice, to growing canes. Unfortunately each of the plants was a weed, and the exotica were thrown willy-nilly on the rubbish compost. It was an honest mistake that I would probably have made, but it was no excuse, and he was banned. I'm not sure it actually bothered him.

For us boys (and girls) the dreaded school certificate examinations arrived in 1941 and we did our best. My latest report from school had indicated that unless I had made up in my own time the homework which I had been excused when firewatching and playing evening cricket, my success could be in doubt. Of course I hadn't made up for the excused homework, there was too much going on. Came the day of the results which the Headmaster would announce at 9.30am, but my father was on duty and met me by the Majestic cinema at the bottom of Halifax Road, as I trundled to school on foot. Unwilling as a snail, to school. But I had passed, he told me, and the crafty devil had called at the *Reporter* offices in Wellington Road at 8am, and checked their list which they had for publication, with a friendly journalist there. He never asked about my friends, to some of whom the result was more important than for me.

"Keff" Sadler duly addressed the form at 9.30 and went through our names alphabetically. Poor Milner, the name before mine, had got four distinctions but failed; the rules were that you must pass at least six (or five) subjects with credits in two or more, something like that. "Keff" looked at me over his glasses and said "Moiser is through" and named whatever I'd got, enough but not much over, and continued "But he didn't do as well as Milner" which quite spoiled my day, though I realised Milner's day was not so hot. I am sure he had another go later on, as we were all quite young for the examination, and passed with ease. I would have said fully 70% of us defeated the examiners and I am sure "Keff" and the masters were proud of us really.

A girl called Olwyn Morris at the Wheelwright Grammar School for Girls also passed this examination, and she later married John Raby, then the curate at St John's, Dewsbury Moor church. He later became Vicar of Claverley, a lovely Shropshire village where I went to live, in 1960 and played cricket for years. Olwyn still had the cutting from the *Dewsbury Reporter* in 1941, showing the pass list, Moiser followed by Morris. It was here in Claverley that I blotted my copy book though. John and Olwyn have a son called David, and I took him with my son, both aged about 8 or 9 to a National Hunt Race meeting at the Woore, near Market Drayton, now long since demolished. The children collected dozens of failed and discarded betting cards, "Honest Joe from Birmingham" and the rest, and being proud of the collection David placed the multi coloured cards around the vicarage dining room mantelpiece. As the Vicar said, afterwards, it wouldn't have been so bad if their guest for dinner that night had not been a local Methodist preacher with strong views on gambling. We did not visit the Woore again, but I do not think the Methodists got it pulled down, it was economically unviable and there was some rationalising of race courses going on at the time, the mid sixties.

Chapter 6

After the school certificate examination, the next academic hurdle was the Higher School Certificate, the equivalent to today's 'A' levels. This could lead to possible university entrance or a better job it was said, but it took two years. They were funny times for academic study in 1941, as the war was not going well for the country and the future looked a bit uncertain, even for a 15 year old. However, I made a start on the higher school certificate work notwithstanding the goings on. Sport continued but with much reduced away travel, and the cadet corps became more prominent, albeit without camps at Filey. A few bombs were dropped on Dewsbury by enemy aircraft and the first landed in 1941 at the bottom of Wakefield Road one night, demolishing two or three houses and killing 8 or 9 people. It was a near miss for the Town Hall. I went to school next morning and was quite surprised to see how far the blast had reached up Leeds Road, where the Co-op shop windows were blown out; that was some four hundred yards from where the bomb or bombs landed. Adam Bird, a young police constable, was first to the scene in Wakefield Road and got some wounded out and then the bodies or parts of bodies that were strewn around. His hair turned grey virtually overnight at that awful experience.

I deemed it right to join the Home Guard, formerly the local defence volunteers, as an under-age fifteen year old. Eyes were closed to my age, but it meant I did not get the nightly subsistence allowance of three shillings and six pence until I was sixteen, nearly a year later, but I learned a lot. This was quite a decision in some ways, because I had to give up my appointment as a company sergeant major in the (non school) Army Cadet Corps for Earlsheaton. This, in fact, was no big deal as the Earlsheaton unit never exceeded 12 or 14 boys, and after drilling them in Earlsheaton Park for 20 minutes, there was nothing else left. It was still Sergeant Major down to Private though, even for "the real thing".

When I first saw Dad's Army on television I knew that was exactly as we were, old men and boys, with a few chaps in reserved occupations and excused service in the ever expanding armed forces. Major Lee, a mill owner was commanding officer and Jimmy Docton was a lieutenant. I never knew whether or not Major Lee appointed himself like Captain Mainwaring but he was like him in build although I have to say a bit more efficient. The headquarters were in the T.A. drill hall near the bottom of Halifax Road, so we did not have to share a church hall with the Air Raid Wardens and Vicar, as they did at Warmington-on-Sea. We guarded the drill hall nightly and assiduously, as we did Whitley. Why Whitley I do not know, but perhaps it had some strategic importance of which I was not aware. It was not conducive to study when once a week, in addition to firewatching and monopoly, there was Home Guard duty which often meant, after parades and drill, standing guard outside the drill hall, 2am to 4am then to return for two hours sleep in filthy blankets (albeit made by Wormalds and Walkers) until 6am when we all "stood down". And that lack of three shillings and six pence a night bugged me too. Most week-ends there were some exercises, defending Whitley again, and there was a time when I would have transferred to Warmington-on-Sea if I had known about it. Our educated member was not a sergeant as in Dad's Army, but Corporal Forrest, an accountant with an office in Bond Street. Again, unlike Dad's Army, the Corporal once slightly criticised me for being on the wrong side of the Wakefield Road cutting on an exercise to defend Dewsbury from the invading hordes approaching from Ossett direction. He was right too, I misread the map. He probably said "You stupid boy", but it was under his breath.

Billy Tremlett's father was reputed to have won an M.C. in WW1 but he was only a private in the Home Guard. He was a journalist, I believe for the *Yorkshire Post*, and had been known to arrive on parade slightly the worse for wear through drink, as did others from time to time. I thought this great fun, but he became a little abusive to all in authority when plastered and any promotion for him was blocked. There was no known procedure for dealing with disruptives in the early days, 1940, (nor in the later days, come to think of it). My father was the senior police officer on duty late one night in 1941 at the Town Hall when a very enterprising officer, not Jimmy Docton, sent another disruptive soldier (he had threatened to thump the adjutant) under escort to the police station. The prisoner and escort were marched in and my father thought it looked a bit odd because the prisoner had the one rifle, at the slope, and the escort, fore and aft, was unarmed. It was pointed out there was a shortage of weapons and one between three was about par for the course at that time. There was nothing my father could or would do except give the disruptive a ticking off and a warning about future conduct, whereupon they all departed, well satisfied with the turn of events; the young officer telephoned his thanks later to my father. We all had rifles by the time I got there, Lee-Enfields. I made a lot of money there (I had to without that three shillings and six pence a night subsistence), on the .22 range in the basement of the drill hall, as we had weekly shooting competitions, by sections or as individuals. It was easy money to me and I picked up pounds in winnings.

Like Captain Mainwaring's men we would have defended Dewsbury, well, Whitley anyway, with results not easy to forecast. My father had very definite and basic views and I was told, as were many other youngsters, that whatever I did, if the Germans landed, I had to kill one German at least before they killed me, for on that basis we had to win as there were more of us than them. Good thinking we all agreed.

There was an anti-aircraft battery at Hanging Heaton, over Caulms Wood, on the (golf course) site, near enough where Sir Alan Cobham and others flew their Tiger Moths in 1935. I was reading Biggles at about that time, and never thought aircraft could fly from Dewsbury, but they did. Alan Cobham had at least three biplanes there and the take off looked a bit scary to me: I was sad that I could not afford the five shillings a time for a flight over Dewsbury, and it was not until many years later that I took my first flight, off Southport sands. "Ikey" Fowler flew from Hanging Heaton, his father coughing up the five shillings, but his father was in trouble with his mother—too risky she thought. The anti-aircraft battery used to bang off at the slightest sign of German aircraft, even over Leeds and Bradford. It did our window frames no good at all, but Bennett Lane suffered more until they all put sticky tape across the windows which saved some broken glass.

The only salvation in all this, to me anyway, was the period, before we became blasé about it all, when we were expected to sit in an air raid shelter at the Leeds Road end of the rugby ground car park during air raid alerts, notified by the horrid siren sounds. Even in the cold and damp of the place, I could sit and admire, even ogle, occasionally chatting up, Annie Heaton, the daughter of the steward and stewardess at the rugby club bar, off the car park via the bowling green. I thought she was the most beautiful and attractive girl I had ever seen but I didn't get very far. Having been attracted to her in the air raid shelter, I often delayed my journey to school to the latest possible bus, so much so I was sometimes late, in order to escort her from the bus, across town to near the shoe shop where she worked, so as to arrive a little before 9am, which did not quite coincide with school start, also at 9am, and a mile away. It was extremely disconcerting, some forty five years later, to find that Colonel Ted Mercer, the sports master at Plymouth College and a former England rugby union trialist, being distantly related to the Heatons, mentioned to Annie by letter my 1941 interest in her, only to find in 1980 she could not even remember me, and didn't know who I was. Any impression I thought I had made was obviously rubbish and this did nothing for my ego.

It was Ted Mercer's uncle, a builder, who con-structed Gawthorpe "Watter" tower, the edifice which still dominates the skyline between Shaw Cross and Ossett. That uncle also had a hand in building Ossett Town Hall, which my cousin Geoff Stapleton, by then a qualified engineer, found to be in a parlous state of repair after WW2, but it was all dealt with and never did fall down to the best of my knowledge. It all shows though that it's a small world.

But back to school and the war, looming ever larger. There was gossip in the cadet corps that if we didn't watch it, the war could be over without our participating. It never seemed to occur to any of us that that might be a good thing. In any event there was talk of conscription to the armed forces at 18, so one or two of the adventurous spirits, with or without the higher school certificate, joined the Indian Army, "Ikey" Fowler and P.K. Emerson for two. Somehow I didn't fancy that even though I was always intrigued by stories of the British Raj, as told by old soldiers of local regiments. I still am, and in moments of fantasy think I was born too late.

What better than early morning char, a parade or two in the early day, lunch in the Mess, a sleep, then a game of cricket (not pig sticking, I could not have done that), gin and tonic in the Mess at sundown, followed by a good dinner; a routine only to be broken by a jaunt up the Khyber every few weeks to put down the latest revolution by the infidels. 'Twas not to be. I was tempted by the Royal Marines who were recruiting at 17 years old. I never heard about the horse marines which tempted some greater men than me, but I liked the sound of what their role was turning out to be. I visited wicked Leeds early in 1942 to join, much to the consternation of my parents, and in due course, after initial welcome, was invited to attend again for a medical examination which was quite thorough and was more than a counting of arms and legs to confirm the right number. I passed and went out and bought a packet of 10 Capstan Full Strength cigarettes to celebrate. I had been told it would be a few months before the country's morale got to such a low ebb that my presence amongst the troops was absolutely vital to the Royal Marines' and my country's well-being, and so it was, as I got my papers to join the corps in Plymouth late in 1942. With that Royal Marines future some months off, it did seem pointless to study more towards the higher school certificate examination, a year or more away, especially as I was, and am, intellectually lazy. So school and I parted on the best of terms; they had done their best for me and I rewarded them with an average performance only, but I have to admit my school reports were often accurate, "He could do much better". On the credit side, I had passed the school certificate examination, I got my colours for cricket and football, passed the certificate A military examination, and had been a prefect, even if not very effective as such. I also knew it was all meaningless if I ended up dead.

What to do with the few months before the real war? I took a temporary job in the Town Hall, under the aegis of the Borough Treasurer, A.E. Richardson, and it lasted the summer of 1942. I was paid at the rate of £78 a year which I thought quite decent, some £6 a month, of which I gave mother £4 a month to help feed and clothe me; she was duly grateful. That few months gave me an insight into the civics of the day and the appropriate committee of the council actually looked at my formal application for a pay rise after a couple of months when I realised the job I was doing, and the pay of my predecessor; alas, considered but refused.

First I had work with rating and valuation of which I understood nothing, and I found out nor did anyone else, but after two or three weeks only I was "promoted" to the wages office, in charge too, to take over from the permanent official, Bill Sowerby, who had been called to the Royal Navy at pretty short notice. It was quite an interesting job for a teenager and I quickly got the hang of it, and soon knew the rates of pay for all the council manual workers from greenkeepers to drivers, from sewage workers to street sweepers and so on. From Wednesday afternoon, the sheets of hours worked by the men (and they were virtually all men) came in from the 8 or 9 council departments, including gas and electricity then. The hours worked up to the previous Tuesday were

then multiplied by the hourly rate to give gross pay. From
that had to be deducted the national insurance stamp
contribution, and income tax, which had some sort of
Pay As You Earn, shortly to be introduced in more detail.
It surprised me that the low paid had an income tax
commitment and I thought it harsh and used my
discretion to lessen the impact when I could lawfully do
that, as I could occasionally. I was working a simplified
"protected earnings" scheme about 25 years before the
state authorised it. All workers had to suffer national
insurance deductions but there were at least 6 or 7
different rates depending on age and sex and hours
worked. When these deductions were added up, the
council employer added his contribution, somewhat
higher as today, and the whole was turned into a cheque,
which I produced at the post office across the road for
the requisite number of stamps which were sticky backed
like postage stamps. These had to be stuck on the
respective employees cards, in the right denominations,
by hand. I never ever balanced those stamps, not because
I was incompetent though I probably was, but because
the workers did not always produce their cards, upon
which their future pensions depended as I repeatedly
told them, to not much avail. The tax deducted was sent
to the Inland Revenue.

When the net pay of all the departments was added
up a cheque was drawn on the Midland Bank, across the
square, for cash which I collected, having worked out,
in round figures how many £1 notes, ten shilling notes
and how much silver and copper I would need. This was
then put into individual pay packets which was very time

consuming and needed extra staff drafted in to help me on Thursdays. It says much for the economics of the day that the cheque for cash was always two thousand pounds or thereabouts to pay the entire council workforce. Of course, this was for manual workers only and I am quite sure the salary bill for the officials and the Education Department, a separate entity, was many times that amount.

Those wage packets were actually taken to the workers personally in the field by three or four of us in taxis on Fridays and whenever possible I opted for the run which included the Lower Laithes sewage works. This always allowed a crossing of the river on a barge which you pulled yourself on the chains, and the excitement of that far outweighed any smell you encountered.

Keith Waterhouse remembered the names of the many Leeds City officials in his youth, whose names adorned notices such as "Keep Off the Grass", "This park closes at 9pm", "Swim only on the Left", Spitting is strictly forbidden" and so on. He was much in awe of those officials, unknown and unseen, as I was, but I then had the advantage of actually seeing some of them. Whilst juniors could not hob-nob with the Bosses, I found they were very human in the flesh. Holland Booth was the Town Clerk, followed by Norman James. Alban Ernest Richardson was the Borough Treasurer as already mentioned, and Arthur (I think) Emerson was the Director of Education; he it was who signed the demands for school fees if your parents were unlucky enough to have to cough up for the offspring's higher education, even at the modest rate of thirty seven shillings and six pence a year. There was a Medical Officer, a Borough Engineer and a Market Superintendent but their names escape me, perhaps because they did not put their names on many official notices.

I hardly came in contact at this time with local councillors or magistrates as I did later, but their names were bandied about in the Town Hall, usually with a reverence not noticeable today. Willie Hooper, of fruit and veg fame, was Mr Liberal but they always seemed to fight losing battles which continued until 1994 and maybe beyond. J.E. Tolson was the Headmaster of Eastborough school and somewhat independent in politics, whilst Kitson Oldroyd was Labour of the old school and none the worse for that. My father said that when Kitson was Mayor, the chief constable, who was nobody's fool, allowed him to use the posh police car for one or two civic functions and Kitson was heard to utter those immortal words "T' moor ah rides i' this 'ere plice motor, t' moor ah laikes it". He would.

The entire Treasurer's department comprised no more than twenty or so bodies and from 1940, as men were moving into the armed forces, it was all left to older men and a few girls. J.L. Dyson was the deputy treasurer, an ex WW1 navy officer of great charm. A Mr Fullerton, of great age then and at his high desk, Arthur Hinchcliffe, Vic Turton, Georgie Read and Florrie Ledgard seemed to run the general office, whilst Terry Bagden and "Black Sam" (so called because he was dark jowled, and needed to shave twice daily) ran the rates office, with a few cashiers and collectors, one of whom was Tupper Winder's uncle. Motor taxation, which dealt with the collection of road fund licence fees and the issue of driving licences, then renewable annually, was dealt with by two people only, a Mr Charlesworth and Rupert Savile, some indication of the lack of motor cars and motor cycles based in Dewsbury.

I doubt the Town clerks' office had very many more, and the mainstays there were Norman Hanson, later to qualify as solicitor on the job, and Percy Bedford, the committee clerk, who I later met in Leamington Spa about 1958 after he had had a break down illness. It was with some sadness that I left this happy band of dedicated and talented clerical workers. What I learned there was of much use in the years to come, and I worked out the "class" system that the council officer workforce took on some of the brightest grammar school leavers who, for one reason or another, did not aspire then to a university education which normally led to better jobs more quickly for the graduates in local government or the Civil Service. Peter Green, Joe Pickup and Billy Speeden were three of that type with whom I worked for those few months.

But off to Plymouth I went, to the Royal Marines, leaving the Town Hall employment before the end of 1942.

Chapter 7

A lot of my school friends like "Ikey" Fowler and P.K. Emerson left our shores for India and stayed away years. My friend, Fred Blackburn, was in the Royal Air Force and left for India in 1943; no-one at home ever saw him again until 1946 when he returned, for demobilisation. I was luckier, in the sense that I had several shorter trips abroad and four or five spots of leave of a few days a time over the almost four years I was away, and I got back to Dewsbury certainly once a year. Nothing seemed to change much during those years, except perhaps there was a touch of war weariness, although there was full employment and bigger wage packets, as overtime pay was easy to come by. Food rationing was there, to stay for several years, and I saw the legal prohibition of conditional sales. A conditional sale was the ability to buy a pair of silk stockings, but only if you also bought two packets of Pasha cigarettes which were revolting, and you did not want anyway. A good thing too, but for some reason elastic was in short supply, and my mother entered certainly one illegal transaction by buying elastic, accompanied by some other useless commodity; this was on the basis that knickers and underpants had to be kept up at all costs.

I finally returned home in May 1946, after another last spell abroad this time in the Mediterranean, and then I thought Dewsbury had changed. There was an air of optimism after so much gloom in the previous five years. Some didn't come back, Tupper Winder for one, and Clarence Wilby, who had indicated at school to his friend "Liddy" Grace and others that he was not going into anything dangerous like the marines or parachute regiment, and opted for the Royal Air Force ground staff, only to be killed on the ground by a sniper in the last few months of the war in Germany. Arthur Turner from Bennett Lane, another wireless operator/air gunner in the Royal Air Force, was also killed on a bombing run over Germany. Some came back a bit the worse for wear, including the window cleaner who lived on the corner of Tinsel Road, opposite my home. He had been a prisoner of war in Japan for some years and I was shocked to see a former upright young man turned into an old man, who slouched along with a shuffling gait and hunched up shoulders, but worst of all he had a horrible yellow colour denoting years of deprivation and worse. His wife, who I think worked in a mill, kept that house going alone whilst he was away and very gradually then nursed him back to some semblance of health. I always "felt" for that couple, so unassuming and nice. There were worse stories than that, of course, but they are just examples.

When I got home I found my father had gone off to Hamburg, where he was in charge of the British Civil Police, under the Control Commission for Germany. He enjoyed that for several years, especially the cheap booze in the mess, until the Commission started to wind down. In fact he flew in considerable comfort to Germany (he would) about 3 or 4 weeks after V.E. Day in 1945, on the very day I came back from Germany by the much more uncomfortable sea crossing. We reckoned he flew over me that day—he would. My mother had by then taken a job in the Borough Treasurer's Office, starting in the Food Rationing Office and graduating upwards to the General Office and stayed there some four years, leaving in 1947 when the "lads" had mostly got back and picked up their local government careers again. My mother was in an age group during the war that could have been directed to work under the government regulations then in force, but worked out it was better to choose her employment rather than be directed somewhere not so pleasant.

I was faced with the prospect of civilian work and I had decided, in conjunction with another marine called Peter Welch from Blackpool, that hard work was not on the cards. The words "leisure industry" had not then been invented but it was down that line we were to travel together. We would start with a modest bed and breakfast place in St Annes-on-Sea, then progress to a small hotel, then a big hotel, then two or three hotels, then a whole chain of them. That, or something like it, was the plan with possible diversions into dance halls and theatres. We were not to do any manual work at all, certainly not, paying minions to do that, but we were to take the cash, organise the bookings even, at a pinch, but mostly plan the next move up the leisure front saga. It was not to be.

Like most young men after an active few years in the forces, I was tempted a little by the outdoor life, and being off women for a reason that now escapes me, I decided I might like to read for a degree in forestry at Newcastle-upon-Tyne University, with a guaranteed job afterwards with the Forestry Commission, likely to be in Scotland. There, I fondly thought, I could lead a bachelor's life of wine and song with my dog, Basher, and slowly watch all the trees I planted grow to perfection over twenty years. I was accepted too, and actually had a rail ticket to go to Newcastle for a preliminary chat with the tutors when my father dropped the bombshell, on a rare home leave visit from Germany.

His friend George Ferguson, he said, was a leading solicitor in Dewsbury and the magistrates' clerk: a member of his staff, Jack Broughton, was leaving to become the magistrates' clerk at Warrington and a replacement was needed. I could see the logic of that but indicated it had nothing to do with me, only to be told that George would like to see me to discuss the possibility of employment with him. I was not impressed, but as my father said, I had nothing to lose and I was not going to Newcastle until the following Friday. This was Tuesday, and against my better judgment I indicated I would go and talk with George about the possibility, only. I said I would make an appointment, but it had been made already for me for 2.30pm that day. Well, I got there and it was a right con job. I came out of that interview firmly believing I was God's gift to the legal profession, as not only would I specialise in magistrates' court work, but I would be given free articles as a pupil solicitor, and that at a time when fathers usually had to cough up £100 or more as premium to the solicitor and the pupil got no pay, except maybe pocket money. On top of that I was to be paid £5 a week for my services. I was sensible enough not to be rushed, but I caved in not much later and accepted it all: it was the £5 a week that did it, as I reckon my father well knew. I returned the railway ticket to Newcastle-upon-Tyne and became an office wallah, albeit within the legal framework. Bang went the open air life of tree growing, and in came hard work studying which I had decided was not for me. How are the mighty fallen.

I started work within days, and used the office in the Town Hall, next to the court, which was old, heavy and oak. A massive dock in court led to the cells in the police station below. It looked impressive. I read a lot about the magistrates' court system, its fairness, its calm dignity, the local magistrates who were drawn from good honest members of society by a system that was secret but effective. All this was written by a man called Leo Page. He was only partly right. The Court sat twice a week, Tuesdays and Thursdays, and usually finished before 1pm, with an 11am start, but there were court sheets to prepare, the listing of names and offences alleged, and then clearing up afterwards, sending out notices to tell people what they had been fined and so on. Those sent to the dungeons needed a warrant, there and then, to authorise the prison governor at Armley Jail to keep the prisoner for x months. But a soft job I thought, overall. George Ferguson, my boss, was a part time magistrates' clerk only, and I only ever saw him on court days which suited me. The rest of his time was spent on his solicitors private practice in Bond Street. He asked me what I thought about office hours, and we agreed 9am to 5pm with an hour for lunch. Saturdays 9am to 12 noon. It was only later I could see why he asked. The pub hours in Dewsbury then were 11am to 3pm and 6pm to 10pm, and a predecessor of mine in the office had fixed his own hours at 9am to 10.55am and 3.05pm to 5.55pm. and would still have been there but for the fact he was walking home along the banks of the river Calder one night, at about 10.15pm, when he fell in and was drowned. Without events of that magnitude, of course, there would have been no subsequent vacancy and I might have been jobless. But I could see the office hours needed a proper footing.

I was greatly assisted in my new job by the Police Warrant Officer, P.C. Wilfred Plumstead, later to achieve very senior rank in the police service. His job was to serve all the summonses which I got issued after they were granted (usually by me, quite wrongly) and execute all warrants of arrest issued by the Court. He also acted as Court Usher on demand, and had another job as well, the Coroner's Officer, succeeding Alan Reid, where he attended post mortem examinations and inquests. It was all quite easy going and relaxed, except when he popped in to pick up his summonses, after attending some grisly post mortem and told me the details. He could help the pathologist by sewing up the cut-up body and so on, for which he got perks of the shillings from the guineas fee. He would recount this, but always ended up by telling me he was going for his breakfast/lunch then, fatty bacon and eggs with fried bread. Oh dear. We became good friends, and he was so perceptive. I had started playing a bit of cricket again for the school Old Boys team, which was quite good quality on occasions, and I had the job of helping Frank Exley and others with selection and notifying the team at one stage. Wilfred shoved his head round the office door and saw what I was doing and insisted on going away and coming back later when the team arrangements were settled. As he said, life was a question of priorities and it was important to know where that priority lay. There was plenty of time for the court work later. We often had a chess game going in the office; it was on top of the safe. I was succeeded in the office later by Sam Gardner, an uncle of Dean Gardner, the then magistrates' clerk after the death of George Ferguson, when I moved to higher things. When Sam went into hospital for a few weeks we even played chess by post, a card moving between us at office and hospital daily, at 1d a time for the stamp. But court. I mastered some of the office intricacies as best I could, and the day came when I was allowed into the court itself to view the proceedings. It would be calm and dignified, as the book said, I thought. Kitson Oldroyd was in the chair with colleagues either side of him and the first case was one of assault, where the man had beaten the living daylights out of his co-habitee, a female. He pleaded guilty, the facts were outlined by the police Deputy Chief Constable, no less, and the man said he was sorry. Kitson did not consult anybody, and in imposing a modest fine, and threatening Armley Jail if it happened again, he ended

"Tha needn't a 'itten 'er that 'ard". The inference I took, as did others, was that she deserved a clout or two for whatever she'd done, but he went fractionally too far. If so, it was well put, but I doubt the court was like that in suburban Surrey, or wherever Leo Page was.

For all that, I later formed the view that Kitson was a good magistrate and not much escaped his eagle eye. Sentencing was much more effective then, due to people like Kitson Oldroyd, Teddy Gundill, the jeweller, and Fred West, the undertaker, and the local villains knew where they stood, not like today where the whole sentencing game is a lottery, even that dominated by the welfare approach, which is where it has all gone wrong, whatever those who wish to see good done say.

It was a good Bench as these things go, and J.E. Tolson was in there fighting his corner. He was also on the juvenile court panel which had been set up in 1933, but in 1946 the Lord Chancellor decided that, the war over and done with, a look should be taken at the courts. He indicated that those over 65 years of age should not deal with juvenile offenders, as there should be a more youthful juvenile court. J.E. Tolson was not only on the Juvenile Court Bench, he was Chairman of it, due to his educational background no doubt, but he was also 80 years old, or thereabouts. He was so good, my boss, George Ferguson, wrote a special letter to the Lord Chancellor asking that J.E., albeit 80ish be allowed to continue for a year or two longer, and that the rules be not applied to him. To my amazement the Lord Chancellor wrote back agreeing, and there he remained for several more years.

I shook J.E. a year or so later, when he fined a farmer at Thornhill fifteen shillings for allowing a cow to stray on the highway. The maximum fine was five shillings per animal. He somehow realised later what he had done and asked me what was to be done. I told him I just sent the farmer a demand for five shillings because I knew what he, J.E. had done was wrong and it was not worth a fuss; I could keep a further ten shillings on the books, and "lose it" over the next few years. I quite ruined his day as I had totally ignored what the Court decided, although he never said what he would have done, or I should have done. I thought the interests of justice had been well served by my enterprise. Today, I suppose I would get the sack, and there would have to be a 2 inch thick file of paper to the Home Office before the Crown granted a Royal Pardon.

The solicitors in town were getting back from the war in various states of health. Dean Gardner, later to become the magistrates' clerk following the untimely death of George Ferguson, came out of the Army as a half colonel after a gruelling time in tanks in North Africa. Neil Jordon had been shot to pieces just about everywhere—a most charming man. Jimmy Matthews came to Chadwick Son and Nicholson and went, but, alas, not before some of us heard his rendering of a Scottish lament, sung in a high pitched tenor. He later became a deputy secretary of the Law Society, the ruling body of solicitors, and a Master of the High Court, a senior type judge. Philip Hallam, later to become a circuit judge, was back safe and sound and spent a lot of time persuading me to get on with my legal studies. He took me for lunch on my first visit to the Bradford Wool Exchange and Liberal Club, and pointed out men who had made half a million pounds in wool dealing, only to lose it all next time around. I had never met that type before. Philip had a delightful house near Royston, and because it was built before 1939 by him, he was not bound to take the "official" electricity, and had his own generator, with petrol ration, which he ran for a couple of hours each night enough to supply the house electricity next day.

I met the old guard solicitors too, Charles Wooldridge, who I knew anyway, as he always read one of the lessons at St Marks Church, living nearby. R.M.A. (Dickie) Kingswell who had played rugby (union) for Yorkshire and was therefore a hero. "Butcher" Thompson was quite different, and really had been a butcher before qualifying as a solicitor. There was some family reason for this but he was most effective and a good lawyer. Except once, when he was having a cigarette with me in my office, instead of being in court, where a man was charged with some serious offence, Mr. Thompson's client being charged with aiding and abetting it. A policeman came out of court and said the first man had been acquitted, whereupon "Butcher" shot into court and, beaming, said that as the first man had been acquitted his client had to be acquitted also, it was as simple as that, and sat down. I have never seen a beam go off a face so quickly when George Ferguson indicated the first chap had not been acquitted at all, but he had been convicted and sent to prison. Woe, woe, woe for

"Butcher" and I came away from the courtroom—I hadn't the heart to see him try and get out of that one.

They were mostly very good advocates, fair and humane, and oozing common sense so lacking often today. I learned a lot from them all, put to good use later on.

Other things moved on. I invested £45 of my war gratuity in a motor cycle and sidecar, bought from an entrepreneur half way down Leeds Road. It wasn't worth £45 but it had a scarcity value as redundant army vehicles had not then appeared on the market. What a motor cycle. It was a P and M actually made at Cleckheaton, and there was no foot gear change, but a gear lever down the side of the tank, 1, 2 and 3. Oh bliss. The prospect of journeys way beyond Ossett was before me. It is true that the tyres had some holes in them, and the sidecar mudguard could come off unless it was handled correctly but she was a goer.

Occasionally I could afford lunch in the "British Restaurant" in the Town Hall (speciality cabbage—ugh) but it was a good value meal (except for the cabbage) for one shilling. I invited my cousin, Geoff Stapleton to lunch one day, as he was then working for Ossett Council. I must say I was a bit miffed when he drove up in a 1923 Singer, I am sure it was, which he had bought, second hand of course, for Twelve pounds ten shillings; not only that, he got a spare engine for the cash as well.

I was just 21 and entitled to the key of the door, never been 21 before, and realised gradually that my growing up was over. Keith Waterhouse only wanted the City Lights, but my contemporaries and I in Dewsbury wanted and got some town lights and a lot of countryside too, even if a few miles out.

I think we were lucky, and I was doubly fortunate, having a stable home, with parents who loved and cared for me. But, from the Rubaiyat of Omar Khayyam, to which I was once headed by Jimmy Docton, although I never appreciated its true meaning or its beauty for another thirty or more years,

> The Moving Finger writes; and, having writ,
> moves on: nor all thy Piety nor Wit
> Shall lure it back to cancel half a Line,
> Nor all thy Tears wash out a Word of it.

If you read a little of the history of Dewsbury, you will find a surprising number of benefactors of the town, which shows somebody was making money out of woollens and rags, if nothing else, and cared enough to provide needed facilities for the less well off. It is not possible to create a full list, it would be too long, but the following are worthy of note in a closing chapter. The Wheelwright Trust provided most of the cash for the two schools to be built, but a further £50,000 came from Dr Matthew Hinchliffe, J.P., who bequeathed it in 1897 for the higher education of boys and girls in Dewsbury, though some went to the Technical School. A Mrs and Miss Fletcher gave £8,000 in 1898 for cottage homes (the Fletcher homes) to be built for married couples or singles of good character who had lived in Dewsbury for 20 years. Alderman William Greenwood left £3,000 in 1934 to build six houses for the poor of Earlsheaton, and they were completed in Town Street by 1936. In 1932,

Councillor J.A. Holroyd gave about fourteen acres of land at Ravensthorpe for a park and recreation ground. Sir Mark Oldroyd gave the turret clock and bells for the Town Hall, built in 1886-89. The stained glass windows were mostly paid for by individual citizens.

These were generous gifts, given the values of the times, and I cannot see them being made again in today's financial and political climate. If that is so, I wonder how much that is due to the abolition of local government exclusively for small compact areas like Dewsbury. A lot I suspect.